Securing the Right to Employment

Securing the Right to Employment

SOCIAL WELFARE POLICY AND THE UNEMPLOYED IN THE UNITED STATES

Philip Harvey

PRINCETON UNIVERSITY PRESS

PRINCETON, NEW JERSEY

Library of Congress Cataloging-in-Publication Data

Harvey, Philip, 1946–
   Securing the right to employment : social welfare policy and the unemployed in the
United States / Philip Harvey.
      p.   cm.
   Bibliography: p.
   Includes index.
   ISBN 0-691-04244-6 (alk. paper)
   1. Public service employment—United States. 2. Public service employment—United
States—Cost effectiveness. I. Title.
HD5713.6.U54H37   1989
362.5'8'0973—dc19   89-30343
                                                                              CIP

This book has been composed in Linotron Caledonia

Clothbound editions of Princeton University Press books
are printed on acid-free paper, and binding materials are
chosen for strength and durability. Paperbacks, although satisfactory
for personal collections, are not usually suitable for library rebinding

Printed in the United States of America by Princeton University Press,
Princeton, New Jersey

For Adolph Lowe

We have accepted, so to speak, a second Bill of Rights under which a new basis of security and prosperity can be established for all—regardless of station, race or creed. Among these are: The right to a useful and remunerative job in the industries or shops or farms or mines of the nation; [and] The right to earn enough to provide adequate food and clothing and recreation.

—Franklin D. Roosevelt, 1944

We're not going to rest, and not going to be happy, until every person in this country who wants a job can have one, until the recovery is complete across the country.

—Ronald Reagan, 1984

I think there will be a lot of water passing through the Mississippi and the Volga before the U.S. Congress and the Administration recognize the American people's right to protection of their social and economic rights.

—Mikhail Gorbachev, 1987

Contents

x · Contents

Tables

Abbreviations

AFDC	Aid for Families with Dependent Children
AFL	American Federation of Labor
CBS	Columbia Broadcasting System
CCC	Civilian Conservation Corps
CETA	Comprehensive Employment and Training Act
CIO	Congress of Industrial Organizations
CWA	Civil Works Administration
DI	Disability Insurance
EAP	Employment Assurance Policy
FERA	Federal Emergency Relief Administration
FICA	Federal Insurance Contribution Act
FSRC	Federal Surplus Relief Corporation
GA	General Assistance
GNP	Gross National Product
NAACP	National Association for the Advancement of Colored People
NIRA	National Industrial Recovery Act
NRA	National Recovery Administration
NRPB	National Resources Planning Board
OASDHI	Old Age, Survivors, Disability, and Health Insurance
OASI	Old Age and Survivors Insurance
PWA	Public Works Administration
SSI	Supplemental Security Income
UI	Unemployment Insurance
WIC	Supplemental Food Program for Women, Infants, and Children
WPA	Works Progress Administration
YWCA	Young Women's Christian Association

Securing the Right to Employment

Introduction

THE RIGHT of all persons to a freely chosen job paying wages sufficient to support a dignified existence has been proclaimed in a number of international human rights agreements concluded since the Second World War.[1] In this country, however, the notion that the right to employment is indeed a human right—like freedom of speech, freedom of association, or the right to be protected from invidious racial discrimination—is likely to be met with some skepticism. We are accustomed to thinking of human rights as synonymous with constitutional rights. It is difficult for us to accept the idea that there may be human rights that are not afforded significant constitutional protection. Indeed, many Americans would undoubtedly dismiss such a claim as alien to our cultural and political traditions, a foreign import from the welfare states of Northern Europe or, worse, from the communist states of Eastern Europe.

In fact, there is a strong entirely indigenous tradition of support in the United States for efforts to guarantee the right to employment. Perhaps the clearest evidence of this tradition is President Roosevelt's 1944 State of the Union message to Congress.[2] Evoking natural rights claims drawn from the Declaration of Independence, Roosevelt characterized the exclusively political focus of the nation's original Bill of Rights as no longer adequate:

> This Republic had its beginning, and grew to its present strength, under the protection of certain inalienable political rights—among them the right of free speech, free press, free worship, trial by jury, freedom from unreasonable searches and seizures. They were our rights to life and liberty.
>
> As our Nation has grown in size and stature, however—as our industrial economy expanded—these political rights proved inadequate to assure us equality in the pursuit of happiness.
>
> We have come to a clear realization of the fact that true individual freedom cannot exist without economic security and independence. "Necessitous men are not free men." People who are hungry and out of a job are the stuff of which dictatorships are made.

To correct this deficiency he called on Congress to give effect to "a second Bill of Rights under which a new basis of security and prosperity can be established for all—regardless of station, race or creed." The first item in his proposed economic bill of rights was "the right to a useful and remunerative job." The second was "the right to earn enough to provide adequate food and clothing and recreation."[3]

Moreover, in expressing the view that society has a duty to secure the right to employment, President Roosevelt was entirely in step with public opinion. Almost 68 percent of those queried in a *Fortune* magazine poll conducted in 1944 supported the proposition that the federal government should, if necessary, assure jobs for everyone seeking work.[4] Even the Republican presidential candidate that year, Governor Thomas E. Dewey of New York, took the position that, "if at any time there are not sufficient jobs in private enterprise to go around, the government can and must create job opportunities, because there must be jobs for all in this country of ours."[5] A quarter-century later, in June 1968 and January 1969, public opinion was again tested on this issue in a Gallup poll that asked the following two questions:

> As you may know, there is talk about giving every family an income of at least $3,200 a year, which would be the amount for a family of four. If the family earns less than this, the government would make up the difference. Would you favor or oppose such a plan?
>
> Another proposal is to guarantee enough work so that each family that has an employable wage earner would be guaranteed enough work each week to give him a wage of about $60 a week or $3,200 a year. Would you favor or oppose such a plan?[6]

The $3,200 figure was the official poverty threshold for a family of four in 1965,[7] and the intent of the questions was evidently to test popular support for both guaranteed income and guaranteed employment schemes designed to provide families with at least a poverty-level income. The guaranteed income proposal was emphatically rejected, 58 percent to 36 percent in the first survey and 62 percent to 32 percent in the second. The guaranteed employment proposal was even more emphatically endorsed, 78 percent to 18 percent in the first survey and 79 percent to 16 percent in the second. What makes these results particularly significant is that neither public policy analysts nor politicians were actively supporting guaranteed employment schemes at the time, while guaranteed income proposals were being vigorously promoted by conservatives and liberals alike.[8] Thus, the expression of public opinion in these surveys cannot be attributed to the influence of a popular president, as those in 1944 might have been. To the contrary, it suggests the existence of a deep and enduring current of spontaneous public support for the proposition that the federal government should guarantee everyone the right to a job paying living wages.[9]

This sentiment has even survived the Reagan era. In a New York

Times/CBS News Poll conducted in late November 1987, the proposition that "the government in Washington should see to it that everyone who wants a job has a job" was supported by a margin of 71 percent to 26 percent. The only proposal receiving more support was that the government should "guarantee medical care for all people." Proposals that the federal government should "uphold traditional moral values," "see to it that day care and after-school care for children are available," "support anti-communist forces around the world," and "put limits on imports of foreign products," all received substantially less support, as did the then recently announced intermediate nuclear force reduction treaty with the Soviet Union.[10]

The notion that it ought to be a duty of government to secure the right to employment is anything but a foreign import to the United States. Indeed, given the broad popular support that the idea has apparently enjoyed in the United States for at least half-a-century, the question that presents itself is why efforts to secure the right to employment have fared so poorly in the legislative process. Twice since 1944 major legislative drives have been undertaken to enact statutory schemes that would have effectively guaranteed the right to employment in the United States, but neither of these efforts was successful.[11]

Still, these efforts did lead to the enactment of statutes declaring it to be a mandatory goal of federal public policy to secure the right to employment. This aim is most clearly stated in the Full Employment and Balanced Growth Act of 1978 (the Humphry-Hawkins Act). In it Congress "declares and establishes as a national goal the fulfillment of the right to full opportunities for useful paid employment at fair rates of compensation of all individuals able, willing, and seeking to work."[12]

Are there good reasons for Congress's refusal to go further than this and enact legislation that would actually guarantee the right to employment? If not, how can Congress's refusal to do so be explained? These are the questions addressed in this book.

In chapter 1 I consider how a policy for securing the right to employment might be structured in the United States. Borrowing the outline of my strategy from New Deal social welfare planners, I term the proposal an employment assurance policy (EAP). Its adoption would require a restructuring of the nation's social welfare system to distinguish between people who need public assistance because they are unable to work (or are not expected to do so) and people who need public assistance because they have no work. The former group would continue to receive gratuitous income transfers under existing social welfare programs. The latter group would be declared ineligible for such benefits but would instead be assured a statutory right to employment in a public sector job paying market wages. Workers who were initially unable to command market wages sufficient to earn a poverty-level income (for instance, unskilled single parents) would be offered special training to increase their earning capacity, but with the guarantee of a job utilizing their newly acquired skills upon completion of their training.

In chapter 2 I define a set of hypothetical parameters for an EAP jobs program that would give effect to this policy. I then estimate what such a program would have cost for the ten-year period between 1977 and 1986. Though necessarily tentative, the conclusions I reach regarding the affordability of an employment assurance policy are encouraging. While an EAP jobs program would have cost more than the social welfare programs it would have replaced, the program's net funding deficit would have been surprisingly small. A 12-percent increase in Social Security tax rates over the ten-year period (from 7.15 percent to 8.05 percent in 1986) would have covered the entire deficit. Moreover, there are good reasons to believe that my estimate overstates what the actual net cost of such a program would have been.

I then turn my attention to the likely effects of an EAP jobs program. In chapter 3 I assess the effectiveness of such a program as a policy response to the closely related problems of unemployment and poverty. I argue that an EAP jobs program would constitute an effective and socially productive response to the distinct challenges posed by different types of unemployment, and that it would also provide superior antipoverty effects compared to current policies.

In chapter 4 I analyze the economic side effects of an EAP jobs program. Some of these would be beneficial and some would not. The most serious problem attributable to the program would probably be its near-term inflationary effect. At the same time, however, I argue that the program would also make it easier to deploy effective antiinflation policies. Indeed, I suggest that the overall effect of the program would be to enhance our ability to fight inflation, regardless of the source of the inflation.

In chapter 5 I examine the administrative problems that such a program would be likely to encounter. It is in this area that the policy raises the most serious questions. Could government officials be prevented from undermining the program's employment effect by using it to replace rather than to supplement existing public sector jobs? Could potential labor relations conflicts with regular government employees be managed? Could useful work be found for the program's workforce? Without minimizing these problems, I argue that they are manageable. I also point out that these problems would be accompanied by extraordinary opportunities to improve and expand the delivery of public services in the United States. Considering all the social benefits likely to flow from an EAP jobs program, it is my contention that the administrative chal-lenges that would accompany such a program are worth facing.

Having drawn the general conclusion that a practical program to secure the right to employment is both feasible and desirable in the United States, I turn in chapter 6 to the question of why efforts actually to secure this right have met with so little success. If realization of the right to employment really is an accepted goal of federal public policy, and if deliberate public sector hiring to achieve that goal really would be su-perior to existing employment and antipoverty policies, then why has such an approach not been tried? I seek an answer to that question in the political history of past efforts to secure the right to employment in the United States. I argue that the political problems that such initiatives have consistently faced are not based on a lack of popular support for the idea of providing employment assurance, but reflect the entrenched po-litical power of special interest groups that oppose the idea. Unfortu-nately, given the continuing strength of these interest groups, I conclude that it is probably unrealistic to expect the right to employment to be secured in the United States any time soon.

Disheartening as this conclusion may be for people sympathetic to the claims advanced in this book, I believe my overall analysis presents a two-pronged challenge to defenders of existing public policy in this area. First, it calls current policies into question on strictly utilitarian grounds by suggesting that a substantial sacrifice in aggregate economic welfare is being endured in this country for reasons that do not bear close scrutiny. At the same time, however, my analysis also raises a human rights issue. If access to a job paying decent wages is a human right, as international agreements proclaim and as President Roosevelt's 1944 State of the Union message suggests, then we are not dealing with a matter of purely discretionary public policy. Viewed as a human rights issue, the question that must be addressed is not whether current policies maximize national income, but whether they are responsive to the fundamental obligations that humanity is beginning to regard as binding on all governments.

Human rights advocates have traditionally devoted almost all of their time and energy to the promotion of civil and political human rights.[13] One of the reasons for this is the uncertainty that surrounds the definition of performance standards for assessing the adequacy of a government's efforts to secure economic and social human rights. Relevant interna-tional human rights agreements generally require governments to do no more than promote the progressive realization of economic and social hu-man rights, while requiring them to guarantee civil and political human rights immediately.[14] For example, state parties to the International Cov-enant on Economic, Social and Cultural Rights promise only "to take steps . . . to the maximum of [their] available resources, with a view to achieving progressively the full realization of the rights recognized in the present Covenant by all appropriate means, including particularly the adoption of legislative measures."[15] In contrast, state parties to the companion International Covenant on Civil and Political Rights promise "to ensure to all individuals within [their] territory and subject to [their] jurisdiction the rights recognized in the present Covenant."[16] Here international law mirrors the United States example, criticized by President Roosevelt, of providing less protection for economic and social human rights than for civil and political human rights.

This poses a problem for those seeking to hold governments accountable for their performance in securing economic and social human rights. How do you assess whether a government's efforts to "promote" a right are adequate? Performance standards are clearly needed, but they are not easy to define. The problem is aggravated when the object of scrutiny is our own government's performance, because the United States is not a party to the international agreements mentioned above and is therefore not legally bound to observe even the very vague performance standards these agreements do impose.[17]

As I have noted, however, the federal government of the United States does have a statutory obligation to promote the right to employment, based on the Employment Act of 1946 and the Full Employment and Balanced Growth Act of 1978,[18] which is essentially the same as that incurred by state parties to international agreements in this area. Thus, the legal duty of the United States with respect to the realization of the right to employment is substantively similar to that of countries that have ratified these agreements.

Human rights advocates need not limit their activities, of course, to the monitoring of a government's record of compliance with the human rights obligations it has formally acknowledged under domestic or international law. The goal of human rights advocacy is not only to ensure that governments live up to their express promises, but to press them to assume as-yet-unacknowledged responsibilities for the protection of human rights. The inherent difficulty of defining standards for the assessment of a nation's performance in realizing economic and social human rights remains the same, however, whether it is the protection of acknowledged or unacknowledged rights that is being monitored.

One way of overcoming this difficulty is to compare the performance of different countries with respect to the realization of particular rights, judging one nation's performance by what other nations at a similar stage of economic development have managed to achieve. Another way is to judge a government by its own past performance, holding it strictly accountable for any deterioration in the protection it affords particular rights and insisting that it demonstrate steady progress in efforts to fully realize those rights.

While both of these methods are worth pursuing, they have limitations. Perhaps the most serious of these is that conditions beyond a nation's control may reasonably prevent it from duplicating either the performance of other nations or its own past performance in realizing certain economic and social human rights, even though the nation's efforts to realize the rights may surpass those of the standard-setting nation or its own past efforts. This problem is likely to be particularly pronounced where the right to employment is at issue because of the inherently cyclical character of employment levels in market economies.

Thus, to properly assess a government's efforts to secure the right to employment, a performance standard is needed that defines the level of protection a nation is capable of affording the right at any given time. One possible way of developing such a standard is to undertake an analysis of whether there are means currently available to a nation whereby it could better realize the right without undermining other legitimate public policy commitments. If such means are available, then the nation might be deemed to have an obligation to match the level of performance that could be achieved through these means, whether or not those particular measures are the ones adopted to achieve this goal.

This method of defining performance standards for the realization of the right to employment has its own limitations. The kind of policy analysis that is needed to develop standards of this type is exceedingly complex. Also, speculative standards are relatively easy to dismiss as unrealistic. It is much more difficult to dismiss performance standards based on actual past or concurrent practice. Still, I believe the effort to develop such standards is worth undertaking. Advocates of conservative economic and legal doctrines have demonstrated the effectiveness of joining economic and legal discourse in pressing a particular social agenda, despite the fact that their claims are often based on purely theoretical analyses of the likely performance of market institutions in a less regulated economic environment.[19] There is no reason why joint advocacy of other economic and legal doctrines should not prove similarly effective, and policy debate regarding the realization of economic and social human rights seems ideally suited for such efforts.

This book can be viewed, therefore, as an experiment in this type of legal argument as well as a straightforward policy analysis of the feasibility and desirability of using government resources to guarantee the right to employment. More precisely, I argue that self-interest alone should direct the nation to adopt measures securing the right to employment, and my study may therefore be regarded as an effort to address the concerns of conventional policy analysis. At the same time, however, it is also possible to view my study as an effort to advance a human rights claim that effective governmental action to secure the right to employment is morally and possibly even legally obligatory in the United States. If it actually would be possible for the United States to secure the right to employment, without ignoring other legitimate public policy commitments, then human rights advocates have strong grounds for pressing the country to do so. My specific proposal need not be adopted, but legitimate demands can be made that effective alternative measures must be adopted.

In other words, the case for recognizing the right to employment can be made strictly on utilitarian grounds, but it need not be limited to such arguments alone. Moreover, if a legitimate human rights claim demanding protection for the right to employment can be made, then both political and moral considerations argue for making that claim as forcefully as possible. Consider, for example, the history of the civil rights movement in the United States. It would certainly have been possible to argue for an end to racial discrimination strictly on utilitarian grounds. Neoclassical economic theory suggests that such discrimination is economically irrational. Does anyone believe, though, that it would have been politically wise for the civil rights movement to have limited itself to such arguments? More pointedly, does anyone believe that it would have been morally acceptable for the country to continue to tolerate slavery, or school segregation, or employment discrimination, if such practices could in fact have been shown to be more "efficient" than nondiscriminatory ones?

The unemployed are a substantially powerless minority in the United States. Experience has shown that so long as unemployment does not threaten too large a segment of the population, very few demands will be made on behalf of the unemployed through the electoral process. Add to this the strength of the political opposition that exists to measures that would secure the right to employment in the United States, and the prospects for securing that right appear very bleak indeed. This political reality will not be altered merely by adding a human rights claim to more utilitarian arguments for securing the right to employment, but efforts to join the two arguments would at least help to sharpen debate over the direction social welfare policy should take in the United States. It could also help to mobilize public support for new initiatives designed to secure the right to employment, thereby extending the horizons of what is politically thinkable in this area.

CHAPTER 1

The Missing Leg of U.S. Social Welfare Policy

IN FORMULATING a strategy for securing the right to employment, the watershed question that has to be answered is whether it is reasonable to rely on macroeconomic policy alone to achieve full employment, or whether a policy of intentional job creation in the public sector is required. In the United States, at least, the historical record suggests that the latter approach is necessary.

It is certainly not impossible for market economies to achieve full employment without intentional public sector hiring and to sustain such a condition for relatively long periods of time. We shall presently see that a number of countries with developed market economies have done just that. The United States has no such record of success in pursuing the goal of full employment, however, and there is no reason to believe that the nation's economy is likely to improve its performance in this regard in the foreseeable future. Indeed, I shall show that the long-term trends are in the opposite direction. In light of this record, any claim that full employment can be achieved in the United States through exclusive reliance on macroeconomic policy (whether interventionist or noninterventionist) warrants considerable skepticism. Those who suggest that the right to employment can be secured in the United States by relying on such means have a very heavy burden of proof to bear. Given the nation's performance record in this area, it is certainly more reasonable to assume that securing the right to employment will require deliberate public sector hiring to provide jobs for those persons unable to find work in the regular labor market. That is what the following analysis attempts to show.

THE HISTORICAL RECORD OF UNEMPLOYMENT IN THE UNITED STATES

The term "full employment" may be used in different ways. It is now frequently defined as the rate of unemployment necessary to keep inflation in check. This is what economists have in mind when they suggest that the economy has in fact achieved or is approaching full employment with an unemployment rate of 5 to 7 percent.[1] If, however, we define full employment as a labor market condition in which the right to employment has been realized, it must mean that enough employment opportunities exist to enable all job-seekers to find a job at wage rates sufficient to support a dignified existence.

This latter definition of full employment was the prevailing one in the 1940s when the term first entered the lexicon of political debate in the capitalist world.[2] For example, in a widely cited book on the subject that was published toward the end of the Second World War, Sir William Beveridge defined full employment as follows:

> It means having always more vacant jobs than unemployed men, not slightly fewer jobs. It means that the jobs are at fair wages, of such a kind, and so located that the unemployed men can reasonably be expected to take them; it means, by consequence, that the normal lag between losing one job and finding another will be very short.[3]

Even according to this definition, full employment does not mean zero unemployment, since even in an economy experiencing a labor shortage it still takes time for job-seekers to complete job searches, and during that period they will be counted as unemployed.[4] Unemployment of this type is termed "frictional" by economists, and it is generally attributed to the existence of imperfect information in the labor market (and the consequent delay that occurs in matching unemployed workers with available jobs).[5]

Thus, in another widely cited study from the immediate postwar period, an international working group of eminent economists led by John Maurice Clark defined the "practical meaning" of full employment as, "a situation in which unemployment does not exceed the minimum allowances that must be made for the effects of frictional and seasonal factors."[6]

The kind of joblessness that would be eliminated with the achievement of full employment (according to this definition) includes what economists generally refer to as "cyclical" and "structural" unemployment. Cyclical unemployment is joblessness attributable to a reduction in the aggregate demand for labor caused by a general decline in business activity. Structural unemployment is joblessness attributable to changes in the technological, industrial, occupational, geographic, or demographic structure of the economy, such that available jobs do not match the available work force in number, location, or type. The pool of cyclically unemployed workers grows during recessions and then shrinks again during periods of economic expansion. Structural unemployment, on the other hand, can persist for very long periods of time and through all phases of the business cycle.[7]

For the right to employment to be secured, both cyclical and structural unemployment would have to be reduced to negligible amounts and any residual unemployment would have to be attributable to bona fide frictional factors. Assuming adequate prevailing wage levels, this probably

TABLE 1.1

Average Annual Civilian Unemployment Rate in Selected Countries: 1959 to 1986 (percent, adjusted to approximate U.S. concepts)

	United States	Canada	Australia	Japan	France	Germany F.R.	Great Britain	Italy	Sweden
Mean Rate									
1959–1986	6.1	6.8	4.1	1.8	4.2	2.6	5.6	3.8	2.1
1959–1974	5.0	5.2	2.1	1.4	2.0	0.8	2.9	3.0	1.9
1975–1986	7.6	8.9	6.9	2.3	7.2	4.9	9.1	4.8	2.4
Median Rate									
1959–1986	5.8	6.4	2.8	1.6	2.8	1.5	3.6	3.3	2.0
1959–1974	5.4	5.4	1.9	1.3	1.8	0.6	3.1	3.0	1.7
1975–1986	7.4	8.2	6.3	2.3	7.0	3.8	8.6	4.7	2.4

Sources: U.S. Bureau of Labor Statistics, Handbook of Labor Statistics, bulletin 2217 (Washington, D.C.: U.S. Government Printing Office, 1985), p. 419 (table 126); and Monthly Labor Review 109–11 (monthly, 1986–88), table 46.

means an unemployment rate of 2 percent or less would have to be achieved (possibly with some additional unemployment attributable to very short-term seasonal fluctuations in business activity).

This is the full employment goal that the Clark study suggests is reasonable,[8] and table 1.1 provides strong empirical evidence that it is indeed a good estimate of the frictional unemployment floor in market economies that are either experiencing very rapid economic growth with limited labor supplies or where very aggressive full employment policies have been successfully pursued.

Table 1.1 shows that for the sixteen-year period between 1959 and 1974, Australia, Japan, France, West Germany, and Sweden all had average unemployment rates of 2.1 percent or less. Moreover, despite the dramatic increases in unemployment rates that have occurred in most of the countries listed since then, Japan and Sweden have continued to enjoy unemployment rates close to the 2-percent level. Based on this record, it seems reasonable to conclude that unemployment in the United States would have to be reduced to a similar level before we could safely assume that all persons looking for work at prevailing wages would be able to find it.

Resistance to the idea that this ought to be our working definition of full employment is sure to be strong among policy analysts in the United States. This is attributable in large part to the already-noted redefinition of the term "full employment" that has taken over in the economics profession during the past several decades. Rejecting the earlier view that the term refers to a labor market condition in which everyone seeking work at prevailing wages can find it in a reasonably short period of time, most economists now think of it as a condition of sufficient laxity in the labor market that price stability is ensured without having to rely on an incomes policy.

It can also be argued, however, that demographic and structural changes in the economy have created a situation where the right to employment could be secured with an unemployment rate above 2 percent. I am skeptical of such claims, but if they are correct, then the net cost of the job creation efforts proposed in this book would be lower than my estimates suggest. My use of a 2 percent full employment figure can therefore be regarded as a conservative gesture designed to ensure that my estimates will be more likely to overstate than to understate the size of the job creation effort needed to secure the right to employment in this country.

Table 1.2 shows that, measured on an annual basis, the United States has achieved a rate of unemployment of 2 percent or less only seven times in the past century—in 1906, 1918–19, 1926, and 1943–45. An unemployment rate under 3 percent has been achieved only nine times. An unemployment rate under 4 percent has been achieved only twenty-four times, that is, in only one year out of four. The nation's average (mean) civilian unemployment rate over the past century has been 7.1 percent. Given the disproportionate effect of the depression years of the 1890s and 1930s on this average, however, the median annual rate is probably a better measure of the nation's typical performance in this regard. The median annual unemployment rate in the United States has been 5.5 percent over the past century.[9]

Nor is the economy's performance in achieving full employment improving. While our avoidance of a major depression since the 1930s has meant that the exceptionally high rates of unemployment experienced during that decade and in the 1890s have been avoided, the likelihood that any particular year will be one of greater unemployment than the historic norm has been increasing. As table 1.2 shows, the median annual rate of unemployment from 1890–1945 was 5.3 percent. Since then it has risen to 5.5 percent, despite the economy's better-than-average performance in the immediate postwar period. Between 1946 and 1959 the nation's median annual rate of unemployment was 4.2 percent. In the 1960s it rose to 4.9 percent. In the 1970s it rose to 5.9 percent, and thus far in the 1980s it has been 7.3 percent. The only two decades in the past hundred years with higher median (or mean) unemployment rates than the 1980s it has been 7.2 percent. The only two decades in the past

It is this historical record that leads me to conclude that it is unreasonable to expect either free market forces or macroeconomic policy alone to secure the right to employment in the United States. The existence of substantial involuntary unemployment in the nation's economy cannot be regarded as an exceptional or purely cyclical phenomenon, nor is it a

TABLE 1.2
Annual Civilian Unemployment Rate in the United States: 1890 to 1988 (percent)

Year	Rate	Year	Rate	Year	Rate	Year	Rate	Year	Rate	Year	Rate	Year	Rate
1890	4.0	1905	4.3	1920	5.2	1935	20.1	1950	5.3	1965	4.5	1980	7.1
1891	5.4	1906	1.7	1921	11.7	1936	16.9	1951	3.3	1966	3.8	1981	7.6
1892	3.0	1907	2.8	1922	6.7	1937	14.3	1952	3.0	1967	3.8	1982	9.7
1893	11.7	1908	8.0	1923	2.4	1938	19.0	1953	2.9	1968	3.6	1983	9.6
1894	18.4	1909	5.1	1924	5.0	1939	17.2	1954	5.5	1969	3.5	1984	7.5
1895	13.7	1910	5.9	1925	3.2	1940	14.6	1955	4.4	1970	4.9	1985	7.2
1896	14.4	1911	6.7	1926	1.8	1941	9.9	1956	4.1	1971	5.9	1986	7.0
1897	14.5	1912	4.6	1927	3.3	1942	4.7	1957	4.3	1972	5.6	1987	6.2
1898	12.4	1913	4.3	1928	4.2	1943	1.9	1958	6.8	1973	4.9	1988	5.5
1899	6.5	1914	7.9	1929	3.2	1944	1.2	1959	5.5	1974	5.6		
1900	5.0	1915	8.5	1930	8.7	1945	1.9	1960	5.5	1975	8.5		
1901	4.0	1916	5.1	1931	15.9	1946	3.9	1961	6.7	1976	7.7		
1902	3.7	1917	4.6	1932	23.6	1947	3.9	1962	5.5	1977	7.1		
1903	3.9	1918	1.4	1933	24.9	1948	3.8	1963	5.7	1978	6.1		
1904	5.4	1919	1.4	1934	21.7	1949	5.9	1964	5.2	1979	5.8		

Summary:	Mean Rate	Median Rate
1890–1986	7.1	5.5
1890–1945	8.2	5.3
1946–1988	5.6	5.5
1946–1959	4.5	4.2
1960–1969	4.8	4.9
1970–1979	6.2	5.9
1980–1988	7.5	7.2

Sources: U.S. Bureau of the Census, *Historical Statistics of the United States, Colonial Times to 1970* (Washington, D.C.: U.S. Government Printing Office, 1975), p. 135 (series D–86); and *Employment and Earnings* (monthly), table A–3.

diminishing problem. It describes the economy's normal state. Without supplemental public sector hiring designed to secure the right to employment, the United States economy cannot be presumed capable of providing jobs at prevailing wage rates for its entire labor force.

It should also be noted that because of the very uneven distribution of unemployment among different population groups and in different areas of the country, even if an average unemployment rate of 2 percent was achieved for the labor force as a whole, significant pockets of much higher unemployment would continue to exist. In June 1987, for example, when the national civilian unemployment rate was 6.1 percent, the unemployment rates in 269 distinct metropolitan areas identified by the Bureau of Labor Statistics ranged from 2.2 percent (in Portsmouth, New Hampshire) to 20.5 percent (in McAllen, Texas).[10] The unemployment rate among black youths between the ages of sixteen and twenty-four with less than four years of high school education was 50.9 percent. The corresponding rate for similarly qualified white youths was 19.3 percent, while the rate for adult male workers with a professional specialty was only 2.2 percent.[11] Thus, even if full employment were achieved for the economy as a whole, direct job creation by the government would probably still be needed to secure the right to employment for particular groups of job-seekers.

UNEMPLOYMENT AND SOCIAL WELFARE POLICY

A failure to face up to this necessity can be detected not only in government employment policy, but in social welfare policy generally. Consider, for example, the changes recently enacted in the federal Aid for Families with Dependent Children (AFDC) program.[12] The AFDC program provides cash income assistance to needy children and a caretaker relative (usually the mother) when at least one of the children's parents (usually the father) is absent from home, incapacitated, dead, or (in some states) unemployed.[13] Jointly funded by the federal government and the states, AFDC benefits vary widely in different states of the country, but the level of support provided is generally well below the poverty line. On a nationwide basis, benefit payments for the typical AFDC family of three averaged $360 per month in 1987, supplemented by an average $200 monthly food stamp benefit. When added together, these benefits provided an average family income equal to only 74 percent of the official poverty line for a three-person household.[14]

In everyday parlance AFDC is commonly called "welfare," though that term is also used to refer to general assistance programs. General Assistance (GA) is a generic term used to describe public relief programs that are wholly funded by state and local governments. Eligibility requirements and benefit levels for GA programs vary even more widely than for AFDC programs. In some states the GA recipient population consists primarily of unemployed single adults. In other states such persons are categorically ineligible for GA assistance. In general, GA programs are conceived as a last resort safety net for the "worthy poor" who are ineligible for other income maintenance programs.[15] On a nationwide basis, total expenditures for GA benefits equal only about 12 percent of total expenditures for AFDC benefits.[16]

Criticism of "welfare" programs has generally focused on AFDC. In recent years this criticism has concentrated on the program's alleged failure to provide adequate incentives for its adult beneficiary population to try to become self-supporting, and on its failure to provide the job training

and work experience necessary for such efforts to succeed. To remedy this defect, Congress and the Reagan administration agreed in the fall of 1988 to a package of significant revisions in the program. Senator Daniel Patrick Moynihan (D–N.Y.), the principal architect of the legislation, has characterized it as an effort to redefine the meaning of welfare dependency. "Receiving income support is no longer to be a permanent or even extended condition but, rather, a transition to employment."[17]

The legislation requires states to establish education and training programs for adult AFDC recipients,[18] and some AFDC recipients will be required to work in exchange for their benefits.[19] To further encourage jobseeking efforts, the legislation also requires states to continue child and health care assistance to recipient families for a limited period of time after they leave the program.[20]

What is notable about this reform package is that it relies exclusively on "supply side" remedies to the problem of welfare dependency. AFDC recipients are to be provided with marketable skills and appropriate incentives to enter the labor market. It is simply assumed that thus equipped and motivated, they will be able to find adequately remunerative employment to support themselves and their children.

This ignores the possibility that the difficulties facing welfare recipients in becoming self-sufficient are rooted more in "demand side" deficiencies in the nation's labor market than in "supply side" deficiencies within the welfare recipient population itself. If job opportunities are plentiful relative to the number of able-bodied persons living in poverty, then a social welfare policy designed to assist or induce the able-bodied poor to enter (or reenter) the regular labor market seems intuitively reasonable. But if job opportunities are not plentiful relative to the need for them, then such a policy is much harder to justify.

This does not mean that a restructured AFDC program designed to enhance the employability of its clients will necessarily fail to place them in jobs. What is unrealistic is to expect such a strategy significantly to reduce the size of the dependent population in need of some form of public assistance. Any regular labor market jobs filled by former AFDC recipients will thereby become unavailable to other unemployed workers. Left unemployed, these workers are likely themselves to become dependent on some form of public assistance, or at least to develop a need for such assistance, whether or not it is provided. With sufficient coaching you may be able to help every loser in a game of musical chairs to win a seat in subsequent rounds of the game, but there is always going to be someone left standing when those rounds are completed. To provide everyone with a seat you have to add chairs to the circle. To end welfare dependency you have to add jobs to the economy.

A proper rethinking of social welfare policy in the United States must rest on a realistic assessment of the job-creating capacity of the nation's economy. As I have argued, such an assessment suggests that policymaking in this area must be based on the assumption that the economy is normally incapable of providing jobs for all those who need them. No other conclusion seems reasonable in light of the record of persistently high levels of unemployment that typify the historical record in the United States, both before and after the federal government began to play an active role in managing the economy. A social welfare policy that ignores this fact while aiming to help the able-bodied poor to become self-sufficient will almost certainly fail. Only if such a policy is combined with a truly effective full employment program does it stand a reasonable chance of success.

This is something that the original architects of the nation's existing social welfare system clearly understood. The overall structure of the system is based on a set of proposals made by a cabinet-level Committee on Economic Security appointed by President Roosevelt in 1934. Chaired by Secretary of Labor Frances Perkins, the committee was formed to make recommendations as to how the nation could best provide its people "some safeguard against misfortunes which cannot be wholly eliminated in this man-made world of ours."[21] In addition to Secretary Perkins, the committee consisted of Secretary of the Treasury Henry Morgenthau, Attorney General Homer Cummings, Secretary of Agriculture Henry Wallace, and Federal Emergency Relief Administrator Harry Hopkins. The committee's recommendations were immediately implemented with the passage of the Emergency Relief Appropriations Act of 1935 in April of that year,[22] and of the Social Security Act of 1935 a few months later.[23]

The point that needs to be made about the social welfare system conceived by the Committee on Economic Security is that it had two legs. The set of income transfer programs established under the authority of the Social Security Act of 1935 put only one of those legs in place, the leg that addressed the economic security needs of those members of society who were either not expected to work or who were only temporarily unemployed. These programs included a joint federal/state unemployment compensation system, a federal old-age pension system, a joint federal/state program of income assistance for children lacking a breadwinner's support (the predecessor of AFDC), and a joint federal/state public health service. The committee also commended the idea of establishing a national health insurance program, but it deferred recommending the immediate establishment of such a program pending more detailed planning.[24]

The system's other leg, indeed its primary leg, was supposed to pro-

vide "employment assurance" to those members of society who were expected to be self-supporting through work.

> The first objective in a program of economic security must be maximum employment. As the major contribution of the Federal Government in providing a safeguard against unemployment we suggest employment assurance—the stimulation of private employment and the provision of public employment for those able-bodied workers whom industry cannot employ at a given time. Public-work programs are most necessary in periods of severe depression, but may be needed in normal times, as well, to help meet the problems of stranded communities and overmanned or declining industries.[25]

The important feature of this part of the committee's plan was that it accepted as given the fact that "employment assurance" could not be achieved through the stimulation of private employment alone. The government would have to supplement the regular demand for labor with a program of public employment designed to be "as nearly like private employment as possible."[26] Nor was the need for such a program perceived to exist only in periods of economic recession.

> In periods of depression public employment should be regarded as a principal line of defense. Even in prosperous times it may be necessary, on a smaller scale, when "pockets" develop in which there is much unemployment. Public employment is not the final answer to the problem of stranded communities, declining industries, and impoverished farm families, but it is [a] necessary supplement to more fundamental measures for the solution of such problems. And it must be remembered that a large part of the population will not be covered by unemployment compensation. While it will not always be necessary to have public employment projects to give employment assurance, it should be recognized as a permanent policy of the Government and not merely as an emergency measure.[27]

Authority to implement this leg of the social welfare system envisioned by the Committee on Economic Security was granted to President Roosevelt in the Emergency Relief Appropriation Act of 1935, under whose authority the Works Progress Administration (WPA) was established in May 1935.[28]

It should not be supposed that these steps were universally welcomed in the United States. There was strong opposition to both legs of the social welfare system that the Roosevelt administration tried to establish, and it was only because of the gravity of the crisis that the nation faced that social innovation on this scale was possible. I shall have more to say in chapter 6 about the unusual political conditions that permitted this kind of experimentation to occur and the opposition that it engendered. Writing in the very different political climate of the 1980s, it is well to

remember just how great the sense of economic crisis had to be for such a fundamental reform of the nation's social welfare system to be possible.

It is also important to note that the sheer size of the nation's unemployment problem in the 1930s, when combined with the strong opposition to government employment programs that did exist, meant that the goal of providing "employment assurance" through the establishment of such programs was not achieved. Jobs were never provided for more than about 45 percent of the unemployed.[29]

With the arrival of full employment during the Second World War, the supplementary government employment programs established in the 1930s were terminated. This step was in full accord with the policy articulated by the Committee on Economic Security that "it will not always be necessary to have public employment to give employment assurance." However, as the war drew to a close, it meant that an entirely new legislative effort was needed if the committee's original plan for a two-legged social welfare system was to be reinstituted. This effort was mounted but it failed.[30] Since then we have tried to walk on one leg only, to hobble along with half a social welfare system.

To recapitulate, the existing social welfare system of the United States was originally based on a two-legged policy. The first leg of the policy was to provide employment assurance to people who were expected to be self-supporting, relying on special government employment programs if necessary. The second leg of the policy was to provide income transfers to needy persons who were not expected to be self-supporting, relying on a variety of federal and state programs to deliver the benefits. During the 1930s both legs of the policy were partially implemented, but the only programs that remained in place following the Second World War were those originally intended to serve people who were not expected to be self-supporting. When Congress refused to restore the other leg of the system, the United States was left with a crippled welfare policy. It certainly would not surprise the original architects of the nation's social welfare system that it has had trouble doing its assigned job with only one of its policy legs in place. What probably would surprise them is that anyone should think that the system's present deficiencies could be cured without restoring that missing leg.

The Fiscal Feasibility of Providing Employment Assurance

THE FUNDING of a public employment program capable of providing jobs for all able-bodied persons unable to find work in the regular labor market would be enormously expensive, but the wages earned by the program's employees would substitute for a broad range of cash and in-kind transfer payments for which such persons are currently eligible. To estimate the net additional cost of providing employment assurance to the nation's labor force, it is therefore necessary to estimate not only the cost of providing the required jobs, but also the savings that would be realized by eliminating the income maintenance benefits that the jobs program would render superfluous. Additional revenues would be needed to implement a policy of employment assurance only to the degree that the cost of EAP-funded jobs exceeded the savings realized from reductions in currently provided transfer benefit payments.

The statistical exercise that follows develops such estimates for the ten-year period between 1977 and 1986. This was a period of unusually high unemployment in the United States. The annual civilian unemployment rate fell below 7 percent only twice, and the average unemployment rate for the entire ten-year period was 7.5 percent.[1] Only during the great depressions of the 1890s and the 1930s has the United States experienced ten-year periods with higher average rates of unemployment.

It will become apparent that this was also a period in which large reductions in government spending for income maintenance benefits were absorbed relative to the number of people experiencing unemployment or poverty. If, during this period, an EAP jobs program could have been wholly or substantially funded from reductions in transfer payments that the jobs program would have rendered unnecessary, then a policy of providing employment assurance can probably be regarded as fiscally feasible in general.

POLICY GUIDELINES

The analysis that follows is based on the assumption that the establishment of an EAP jobs program would be accompanied by a restructuring of the nation's existing social welfare system. To avoid certain estimation problems, this restructuring has been assumed to embody two clear and simple policy principles that probably would not be adopted in pure form in practice. Interestingly, these two principles are drawn from opposite ends of the political spectrum. The first is that the government would henceforth refuse to provide gratuitous income maintenance assistance to able-bodied persons of working age and their dependents—no more welfare, no more food stamps, no more unemployment insurance, no more anything. The second principle is that the government would, as a substitute for the terminated aid, henceforth guarantee employment at living wages to every man, woman, and youth in the country who is unable to find adequately remunerative work in the regular labor market.

In keeping with these principles, the following program parameters have been assumed to apply. First, it has been assumed that eligibility for EAP-funded jobs would be extended to all persons unable to find work in the regular labor market. In other words, eligibility for EAP-funded jobs would not be subject to either a means test or a waiting period. Anyone wanting to work would be guaranteed a job. Second, it has been assumed that EAP-funded jobs would pay wages sufficient to provide a family income at least equal to the official poverty line. Third, it has been assumed that eligibility for all gratuitous income transfer benefits provided by the government would henceforth be limited to the elderly, the disabled, and to children lacking the support of both their parents.

As suggested above, some modification of these program parameters would probably be desirable in practice. For example, a strong argument can be made that it makes good sense to support the short-term unemployed through an unemployment insurance system rather than through a program of public employment. This was the position adopted by the Committee on Economic Security in recommending the establishment of such a system in 1935.

> We believe it is desirable that workers ordinarily steadily employed be entitled to unemployment compensation in cash for limited periods when they lose their jobs. It is against their best interests and those of society that they should be offered public employment at this stage, thus removing them from immediate consideration for reemployment at their former work. Very often they will need nothing further than unemployment compensation benefits, for they will be able to reenter private employment after a brief period, but if they are unable to do so and remain unemployed after benefit rights are exhausted, we recommend they should be given, instead of an extended benefit in cash, a work benefit—an opportunity to support themselves and their families at work provided by the Government.[2]

In keeping with this plan, the nation's existing Unemployment Insurance system (UI) could be maintained as an adjunct to a policy of providing employment assurance.

A strong argument can also be made that it is in the best interests of society to provide enough cash support to the families of very small children to allow a parent the option of remaining at home with them instead of having to seek outside employment (with its attendant necessity of having to arrange substitute child care arrangements). In contrast to the continued provision of unemployment insurance, this goal would not be an easy one to achieve. Given the inadequacies and unpopularity of the existing Aid To Families With Dependent Children program (AFDC), an entirely new program would probably have to be devised before broad public support for such payments could be secured.

For the purposes of the following estimation exercise, however, it has been assumed that neither the parents of young children nor temporarily unemployed workers would be eligible for any government-funded income transfer benefits. In other words, it has been assumed that UI would be entirely supplanted by the government's offer of assured employment, and that AFDC would be reduced to negligible proportions by limiting benefits to families in which both parents were either deceased, incapacitated, or absent from home.

The adoption of this assumption simplifies the task of estimating the net cost of an EAP jobs program, but it also lends an upward bias to the estimate. This is because UI and AFDC benefit levels are generally well below what it would cost to pay and equip an EAP job-holder. Thus, unless large numbers of current UI and AFDC recipients could afford to remain unemployed following the termination of their benefits and would prefer to do so rather than to accept EAP-funded jobs, then an employment assurance policy that allowed for continued payments of these benefits would cost less than one that ended them. In the following estimates, however, a very high job acceptance rate has been assumed for current UI and AFDC beneficiaries, an assumption that tends to discount the possibility that the termination of these benefits would actually reduce the net cost of providing employment assurance to the nation's workforce. The upward bias that the benefit termination assumption introduces into the estimates has therefore been preserved.

THE BUDGETED COST OF AN EAP JOBS PROGRAM

The annual wage bill of an EAP jobs program would depend on (1) the average number of persons needing work during the year, (2) the program participation rate of those persons, and (3) their average wages. I shall address each of these issues in turn.

Likely Candidates for EAP-Funded Jobs

The most likely candidates for employment in an EAP jobs program would be persons who are out of work and actively seeking it, that is, persons now counted as officially unemployed. There are three other groups, however, from which significant participation could also be expected. The first consists of so-called "discouraged workers." These are people who say they want to work but are not actively looking for jobs because they believe none are available for which they could qualify. The existence of an EAP jobs program would probably induce many such persons to join the laborforce.

The second group consists of able-bodied AFDC parents not already counted in the labor force. As previously noted, the estimates that follow are based on the assumption that income maintenance payments would no longer be available to such persons. Most would therefore have little choice but to join the laborforce. This would add to the ranks of the officially unemployed and thereby to the ranks of those likely to take jobs in an EAP jobs program.

The third group consists of involuntary part-time workers who do not normally work full-time. These are people who are working part-time not by choice but because they either cannot find full-time jobs or because business conditions are such that their employers normally give them less than thirty-five hours of work per week. An EAP jobs program would offer these workers an opportunity either to work full-time in an EAP-funded job or to work part-time in the program to supplement their existing part-time employment. There are also involuntary part-time workers who normally work full-time but who have had their hours of work temporarily cut. These workers (about a third of all involuntary part-time workers) would be much less likely to take jobs in an EAP jobs program, and those who did would free up positions that some wholly unemployed persons seeking full-time work would probably find satisfactory.

It is these three groups, then, in addition to the officially unemployed, who constitute the population from which candidates for EAP-funded jobs would likely come. The establishment of an EAP jobs program might affect laborforce participation rates more generally, of course, but the extent and even the likely direction of such an effect is hard to gauge. On the one hand, the establishment of such a program would induce some people to leave the laborforce who are presently in it. Among persons currently working or looking for work there are certainly some who are doing so only because another family member is unemployed or because they fear what would happen if another family member were to become unemployed. Such people might very well choose not to work if their family's primary wage-earner or wage-earners were assured of uninterrupted employment. On the other hand, the program would induce some people to join the laborforce who presently indicate no desire for a job. Some students would choose to work instead of continuing their education. Some housewives would choose to work who would not otherwise consider it a possibility. Since the net effect of these shifts is so uncertain, it seems advisable to disregard them, focusing attention instead on those groups whose response to an EAP jobs program would be more predictable, that is, officially unemployed workers, AFDC parents not already in the laborforce, discouraged workers, and involuntary part-time workers who usually work part-time.

In table 2.1 I show the average number of persons falling into each of these categories on an annual basis between 1977 and 1986. Taking the ten-year period as a whole, officially unemployed workers constituted about 56 percent of the total population of likely candidates for an EAP jobs program. Discouraged workers constituted the smallest group, accounting for only 8 percent of the total, with AFDC parents accounting for another 15 percent. Involuntary part-time workers accounted for about 21 percent of the total, but their relative importance increased substantially over the course of the period. In 1977 they represented less than 17 percent of the population of likely jobs program participants, but following the 1980–82 recession, their share of the total increased to 25 percent. The relative importance of the three other groups of likely program participants all decreased.

Program Participation Rates

An EAP jobs program would not have needed to provide work for everyone identified in table 2.1. First, the existence of an EAP jobs program would probably have had some countercyclical effect. An EAP jobs program would be an exceedingly powerful automatic stabilizer, increasing and decreasing government expenditures at appropriate times to soften recessions, ensure vigorous recoveries, and reduce inflationary pressures at the peak of the business cycle. Even if no net change in aggregate government spending occurred over the course of the cycle, the superior timing of the EAP fiscal mechanism, compared to the fiscal effect of the income maintenance programs it would replace, should flatten the cycle. Thus, relying on historic unemployment data to estimate the number of EAP positions needed to achieve full employment probably overstates the actual size of the job deficit such a program would have to fill. Because of its uncertain size, I have decided to ignore this countercyclical effect in estimating the number of jobs an EAP jobs program would have needed to provide during the ten-year period at issue, but it should be noted

TABLE 2.1
Likely Candidates for EAP-Funded Jobs: 1977 to 1986 (in thousands, except for unemployment rate)

	1977	1978	1979	1980	1981	1982	1983	1984	1985	1986
Total EAP Jobs Program Candidates	12,349	11,289	11,118	13,311	14,545	17,881	18,560	15,899	15,401	15,271
Unemployed Persons	6,991	6,202	6,137	7,637	8,273	10,678	10,717	8,539	8,312	8,237
Others	5,358	5,087	4,981	5,674	6,272	7,203	7,843	7,360	7,089	7,034
AFDC Parents Not in Laborforce	2,253	2,212	2,204	2,331	2,408	1,952	2,031	2,046	2,034	2,065
Discouraged Workers	1,026	863	771	993	1,103	1,568	1,641	1,283	1,204	1,121
Involuntary Part-time Workers	2,079	2,012	2,006	2,350	2,761	3,683	4,171	4,031	3,851	3,848
Official Unemployment Rate (percent)	6.9	6.0	5.8	7.0	7.5	9.5	9.5	7.4	7.1	6.9

Sources and Assumptions: See Appendix.

that this introduces a possibly substantial upward bias into my estimate of the program's cost.

A second reason an EAP jobs program would not have needed to provide work for everyone identified in table 2.1 is because of the previously noted fact that some frictional unemployment is unavoidable even in a fully employed economy. In the estimates that follow, I have assumed that a frictional unemployment floor of 2 percent exists in the United States. In other words, I have assumed that an EAP jobs program would have needed to create only enough jobs to reduce the unemployment rate to 2 percent. In fact, this estimate of the number of jobs such a program would have been required to create may still be too high. Many economists would regard a 2-percent full employment goal as unreasonably low. If they are right and the frictional unemployment floor in the United States is significantly above the 2-percent level, then another possibly substantial upward bias exists in my estimate of the program's likely size and cost.

A third reason an EAP jobs program would not have needed to provide work for everyone identified in table 2.1 is because not all discouraged workers and AFDC parents would choose to join the laborforce even if jobs were plentiful and income maintenance benefits were terminated. While the establishment of an EAP jobs program would certainly induce many discouraged workers to join the laborforce, it is very unlikely that all such persons would do so. A study of discouraged workers completed in 1984 found that about two-thirds had been out of the laborforce for more than a year at the time they reported themselves as wanting a job, and about the same proportion were still out of the laborforce a year later. More significantly, of the two-thirds who had not rejoined the laborforce within a year, almost three-fourths no longer reported themselves as wanting a job.[3]

While there is no reason to doubt the sincerity of the desire for work expressed by discouraged workers, it must be recognized that it is a more tenuous desire than one expressed by people who are actively seeking employment. A possible reason for this is suggested by the group's demographic profile. Though youthful dropouts from the laborforce attract the most attention in discussions of the phenomenon of "discouragement," by far the largest group of discouraged workers consists of women between the ages of twenty-five and fifty-nine, and the next largest group consists of men in the same age group.[4] These cohorts probably include large numbers of housewives and partially disabled adults who are not under strong economic compulsion to seek wage employment. Their families might benefit from having another source of income. They might benefit from having their own income. Still, seeking wage employment is an option they can choose not to pursue.

Because of the weak links that most discouraged workers have to the labor market, any estimate of their laborforce participation following the establishment of an EAP jobs program is largely conjectural. I have assumed that 50 percent of such persons would join the laborforce. According to the study of discouraged workers mentioned above, this is the approximate proportion of all such persons who have either been out of the laborforce for less than a year or who still report themselves as wanting work a year hence. I have further assumed that the proportion of discouraged workers seeking full-time as opposed to part-time work would be the same as for officially unemployed workers. These estimates may be high or low, but because discouraged workers represent a relatively small group in my calculations, a different set of assumptions would not have much effect on my overall estimate of the cost of an EAP jobs program.

The effect of an EAP jobs program on the laborforce participation rate of able-bodied AFDC parents is less uncertain. If such persons were no longer eligible for income maintenance benefits, they would have little choice but to seek wage employment. This does not mean that their laborforce participation rate would equal 100 percent, especially over the long run. AFDC rolls are fed by family instability, and there is little doubt that unemployment contributes to that instability. Indeed, William Julius Wilson has recently argued that increasing unemployment and consequent declines in the laborforce participation of black males provides the best explanation for the growing predominance of female-headed families among the black "underclass."[5] In contrast, by shielding families from the disrupting effects of unemployment, the existence of effective full employment would probably promote family stability, thereby reducing the number of families who would otherwise become candidates for AFDC assistance. Since parents who live together as a family are less likely to need and seek two jobs (especially two full-time jobs), the establishment of an EAP jobs program as a substitute for current AFDC benefits would probably reduce the number of single parents needing either transfer payments or full-time employment. Moreover, even under existing conditions a complete termination of income maintenance benefits for able-bodied AFDC parents would not result in all such persons joining the laborforce. Some would avoid that necessity by relying on relatives or friends for support or by sharing household responsibilities with them.[6]

Recognizing that most, but not all, AFDC parents would be likely to seek work following the termination of their benefits, I have arbitrarily assumed that 90 percent of such persons would enter the laborforce. While this estimate is purely conjectural, it is close enough to the absolute participation limit of 100 percent that it cannot significantly understate what the actual laborforce participation rate of former AFDC parents would be. In other words, if the assumption introduces a significant error into my overall estimate of program cost, it would have to be one of overstatement.

I have further assumed that the proportion of all such persons seeking full-time as opposed to part-time employment would also be 90 percent. This is somewhat higher than the proportion of full-time workers among employed women who maintain families,[7] but the latter group are presumably less needy, on the average, than AFDC parents, and they also include an unknown number of involuntary part-time workers.

Thus, to estimate the number of jobs that an EAP jobs program would have needed to provide for wholly unemployed persons between 1977 and 1986, I added the above stated proportions of discouraged workers and AFDC parents not already counted in the laborforce to the nation's officially reported unemployment figures. I then calculated the number of jobs an EAP jobs program would have needed to create annually between 1977 and 1986 to reduce unemployment in this augmented laborforce to the 2-percent level.

The participation of involuntary part-time workers in an EAP jobs program would have been limited by factors analogous to those mentioned in reference to the other three groups of program candidates. Even if all involuntary part-time workers actively sought either full-time work or supplementary part-time work, frictional underemployment would exist within the group for the same reason that frictional unemployment exists among wholly unemployed workers. Also, not all involuntary part-time workers would become active job-seekers. Such workers might like their present work and be hesitant to either give it up or combine it with a second part-time job, even though they would prefer to work full-time. Also, since involuntary part-time workers are at least partially employed, they have less time to pursue a vigorous job search and are probably under less economic and psychological pressure to do so. Thus, an EAP jobs program would probably have to provide proportionately fewer positions for involuntary part-time workers than for wholly unemployed persons. Taking these factors into account, but having no data to support a more precise estimate, I have arbitrarily assumed that the EAP job acceptance rate among the involuntary part-time workers counted in table 2.1 would have been 75 percent of that assumed for wholly unemployed persons.

I have also assumed that all of the program positions filled by involuntary part-time workers would have been part-time ones, that is, second jobs. In reality, of course, many involuntary part-time workers would have chosen to work full-time in an EAP-funded job if given the chance. In doing that, however, they would have created part-time vacancies in the regular labor market for persons seeking part-time work. The net result would be that an EAP jobs program would have needed to create fewer jobs than the estimates below suggest, but the total number of hours of work provided by the program would have been the same. That is, fewer positions would have been needed, but a higher proportion of them would have been full-time ones.

In table 2.2 I provide estimates of the number of jobs that an EAP jobs program would have needed to provide on an annual basis between 1977 and 1986, given all of the foregoing assumptions. The totals vary from a low of 7.4 million jobs in 1979 to a high of 13.6 million jobs in 1983, with an annual average of 10.2 million jobs. The number of full-time equivalent jobs in this total would have averaged 8.6 million. As I have repeatedly emphasized, the upward bias implicit in many of the assumptions underlying the table's construction means that these estimates probably overstate the number of jobs that an EAP jobs program would actually have been called on to provide.

Wage Rates

How much would it have cost to provide the number of EAP funded jobs shown in table 2.2? That, of course, would depend upon the program's average hourly wage rate and average work week. A number of program policies are conceivable with respect to average wage rates, ranging from an expansive commitment to pay wages equivalent to those available in the regular labor market to a more modest commitment to pay either the statutory minimum wage or wages calculated to match the official poverty line. If the goal of an EAP jobs program is to provide a close substitute for regular employment, then a commitment to pay market wages is clearly preferable. Such a program would be more expensive, though, than one which merely aimed to provide the unemployed with a "security wage."[8]

The total earnings of program participants would also depend on the number of hours of work they were provided. One way of holding down the cost of an employment program while still paying prevailing hourly wage rates is to limit the program's average work week. This formula was frequently adopted in New Deal employment programs.

To obtain a high estimate of the cost of an EAP jobs program, and because it is the policy that best conforms to the programmatic goals outlined by the Committee on Economic Security, I have assumed that program participants would be paid market wages and that they would be offered a full forty hours of work per week, with part-time employees in EAP-funded jobs averaging half that.[9] By market wages I mean wage rates equivalent to those program employees could reasonably expect to earn in jobs obtained through the regular labor market, if such jobs were available.

TABLE 2.2
Number of EAP Jobs Needed to Achieve Full Employment: 1977 to 1986 (in thousands, except unemployment rate)

	1977	1978	1979	1980	1981	1982	1983	1984	1985	1986
Total Jobs Needed	8,685	7,641	7,448	9,391	10,372	13,127	13,640	11,040	10,593	10,441
For Officially Unemployed Persons	5,474	4,676	4,566	5,980	6,569	8,820	8,863	6,712	6,458	6,351
Full-time Jobs	4,324	3,647	3,561	4,904	5,387	7,409	7,534	5,571	5,296	5,144
Part-time Jobs	1,150	1,029	1,005	1,076	1,182	1,411	1,329	1,141	1,162	1,207
For Discouraged Workers	402	326	287	388	438	648	678	505	468	432
Full-time Jobs	318	254	224	318	359	544	576	419	384	350
Part-time Jobs	84	72	63	70	79	104	102	86	84	82
For AFDC Parents	1,588	1,501	1,476	1,643	1,721	1,377	1,512	1,447	1,423	1,433
Full-time Jobs	1,429	1,351	1,328	1,479	1,549	1,239	1,361	1,299	1,281	1,290
Part-time Jobs	159	150	148	164	172	138	151	148	142	143
For Involuntary Part-time Workers (second jobs)	1,221	1,138	1,119	1,380	1,644	2,282	2,587	2,376	2,244	2,225
Official Unemployment Rate (percent)	6.9	6.0	5.8	7.0	7.5	9.5	9.5	7.4	7.1	6.9

Sources and Assumptions: See Appendix.

This does not mean that individual program participants would necessarily receive a wage equal to the last one they earned before becoming unemployed. Workers whose last employment was in a position that paid wages above the prevailing norm for work of that type would not, by virtue of that fact, be paid more than other similarly skilled workers who had not been so fortunate in their former jobs. The program's goal would be to employ individual job applicants in positions that took full advantage either of their existing skills or of their capacity to acquire new ones, and to pay them wages equivalent to those normally offered for similar work in the regular labor market. In other words, the program's wage policy would be similar to the one commonly regarded as appropriate for the setting of public sector wage rates in general. Indeed, the program could simply adopt existing government wage schedules for comparable jobs.

The last wage actually earned by unemployed workers is probably the best indicator of their average earning capacity in the regular labor market. Unfortunately, information regarding the last wage earned by unemployed workers is not regularly collected and published, but it can be estimated based on information obtained from a special survey conducted by the Census Bureau in May 1976.[10]

The mean value of the last wage earned by unemployed workers in that survey was $3.73 an hour.[11] Given the average duration of unemployment at the time, that wage applied to a period about four months earlier, when the average earnings of nonagricultural production workers was $4.72 per hour.[12] Thus, workers who were unemployed in May 1976 had last earned a wage equal to about 79 percent of the average hourly earnings of all nonagricultural production workers. I have assumed that this relative figure represents the average wage that officially unemployed workers could reasonably expect to earn in jobs obtained through the regular labor market and, hence, in EAP-funded positions as well. In other words, I have used a figure equal to 79 percent of the average hourly earnings of all nonagricultural production workers as my estimate of the average wage that officially unemployed workers would be paid in an EAP jobs program paying market wages.

Since the average unemployment rate between 1977 and 1986 (7.4 percent) was almost identical to the May 1976 rate of 7.3 percent, this estimate is probably not significantly biased when applied to officially unemployed workers over the ten-year period as a whole. On the other hand, it probably is biased when applied to individual years in which the average unemployment rate diverged significantly from the ten-year norm. During a recession, the jobless population is swollen with large numbers of cyclically unemployed workers laid off from relatively good jobs. Thus, as unemployment rates rise, the last wage earned by the average unemployed worker is also likely to rise. This means that my estimate of the last wage earned by officially unemployed workers is probably too low for those years during which the average unemployment rate was greater than it was in May 1976, while it is probably too high for those years during which the average unemployment rate was lower than it was in May 1976.

In any case, this estimate of earning capacity applies only to officially unemployed workers. The average earning capacity of the other three categories of likely candidates for EAP jobs is almost certainly less than this. For example, the actual median hourly earnings of all part-time workers in the United States averaged only about two-thirds as much as the average hourly rates that I have assumed an EAP jobs program would have paid to officially unemployed workers.[13] There is no reason to believe that the average earning capacity of discouraged workers, AFDC parents, and involuntary part-time workers would have been significantly greater than that of the general population of employed part-time workers. I have therefore adopted the median wage earned by employed part-time workers as my estimate of the average wage that an EAP jobs program would have paid to discouraged workers, former AFDC parents, and involuntary part-time workers.

In table 2.3 I show the average hourly wage rates that an EAP jobs program would have paid, according to these assumptions. In 1986, for example, the average hourly rate for officially unemployed persons would have been $6.92 per hour (about $14,400 per year), while the average for other program participants would have been $4.63 per hour (about $9,600 per year). The overall hourly rate shown in the table is the weighted average of the rates for officially unemployed persons and for all other program participants, taking into consideration the average number of hours that I have assumed each group would work. In other words, it is an estimate of the average rate that the program would have paid to all EAP job-holders on an hourly basis. In 1986, this average rate would have been $6.16 per hour (about $12,800 per year). For purposes of comparison, the table also shows the federal statutory minimum wage, presumably the lowest rate that would have been paid for any EAP-funded job. In 1986 this statutory minimum was $3.35 per hour (about $7,000 per year).

So far I have ignored the issue raised by the fact that jobs paying market wages may not provide even a minimally adequate income for workers with dependent children. In table 2.4 I show the annual income that a full-time worker would earn at the wage rates listed in table 2.3 compared to the federal government's official poverty thresholds for households of various sizes. Most importantly, the figures illustrate the steady decline in the real value of the nation's statutory minimum wage that has

TABLE 2.3
Average EAP Wage Rates and Statutory Minimum Wage Rates: 1977 to 1986 (in dollars)

	1977	1978	1979	1980	1981	1982	1983	1984	1985	1986
Average Hourly EAP Wage Rate	3.65	3.93	4.26	4.66	5.03	5.47	5.67	5.82	6.00	6.16
Average for Officially Unemployed Persons	4.15	4.50	4.87	5.26	5.73	6.07	6.34	6.57	6.77	6.92
Average for All Other Program Participants	2.68	2.90	3.13	3.41	3.57	3.88	4.04	4.30	4.44	4.63
Federal Statutory Minimum Wage	2.30	2.65	2.90	3.10	3.35	3.35	3.35	3.35	3.35	3.35

Sources and Assumptions: See Appendix.

TABLE 2.4
Annual Income Earnable at EAP Wage Rates and Poverty Thresholds by Household Size: 1977 to 1986 (in dollars)

	1977	1978	1979	1980	1981	1982	1983	1984	1985	1986
Annual Full-time Income at Average EAP Wage	7,597	8,180	8,852	9,696	10,466	11,383	11,797	12,109	12,481	12,809
Average for Officially Unemployed Persons	8,632	9,360	10,130	10,941	11,918	12,626	13,187	13,666	14,082	14,394
Average for All Other Program Participants	5,574	6,032	6,510	7,093	7,426	8,070	8,403	8,944	9,235	9,630
Annual Full-time Income at Minimum Wage	4,186	5,512	6,032	6,448	6,968	6,968	6,968	6,968	6,968	6,968
Poverty Thresholds by Household Size										
One Person	3,075	3,314	3,689	4,190	4,620	4,901	5,061	5,278	5,469	5,572
Two Persons	3,951	4,244	4,725	5,363	5,917	6,281	6,483	6,762	6,998	7,138
Three Persons	4,833	5,201	5,784	6,565	7,250	7,693	7,938	8,277	8,573	8,737
Four Persons	6,191	6,662	7,412	8,414	9,287	9,862	10,178	10,609	10,989	11,203

Sources and Assumptions: See Appendix.

occurred since it was last increased in 1981. At the end of the 1970s a minimum-wage job could generate an income above the poverty threshold for a three-person household. By 1986, the real value of the minimum wage had declined to the point that it was no longer capable of providing an income above the poverty threshold for even a two-person household.

The poverty threshold for a three-person household is especially important, because that is the size of the average AFDC family,[14] and AFDC parents must be presumed to include many persons whose current earning capacity is at the minimum wage level. In those situations where a minimum-wage job would be inadequate to generate even a poverty-line income, then humanitarian considerations would strongly urge us to pay wages above the statutory minimum.

If the statutory minimum wage had been maintained at its historic levels, of course, the number of EAP job-holders in need of such special consideration would have been very small. During the 1950s and 1960s the federal minimum wage was generally maintained at a level equal to about 50 percent of the average hourly earnings of nonagricultural production workers.[15] An equivalent minimum wage in 1986 would have been $4.38 per hour. This would have generated an annual income of $9,110, a figure just above the poverty threshold for a family of three.

Even with an increase in the statutory minimum wage, there would be some minimally skilled EAP candidates with large families who would have to be paid an above-market wage to receive a poverty-line income. One way of doing this would be to give such workers preferential consideration for higher paying EAP positions for which they are qualified (like veterans preferences for civil service hiring). Individuals lacking the skills necessary to perform in such positions could be targeted for special training programs, while individuals with nonremediable occupational handicaps could be employed in "sheltered workshop" programs (where a non-market wage policy could be followed without raising serious pay equity concerns).

Alternatively, of course, parents earning less than a poverty-line wage could be provided with cash or in-kind income supplements modeled on either the earned income tax credit or the food stamp program, but that would run counter to my assumption that able-bodied persons of working age would no longer be eligible for uncompensated income maintenance benefits.

Finally, it should be recognized that some people would question the need to guarantee a poverty-line income to EAP job-holders. As I noted in chapter 1, combined AFDC and food stamp benefits are currently well below that level. On the other hand, both the public opinion data reported in the introduction to this book and the history of federal minimum wage legislation suggests that it would probably be easier to win public support for a jobs program that guaranteed at least a poverty-level income than to increase transfer payments to that level. In any case, an EAP jobs program that guaranteed unskilled workers with dependent children a poverty-line wage is certainly conceivable, especially if the statutory minimum were maintained at its historic levels.

One formula that could be adopted to achieve this end would be to guarantee workers with dependent children a minimum full-time wage at least equal to the official poverty threshold for a household consisting of the worker and any dependent children residing in the same household, but not including other able-bodied adults with whom the worker might also reside. This would ensure that single parents have the opportunity to earn at least a poverty-line family income, and if both parents in a two-parent household were allowed the benefit of the rule, they could earn a joint income substantially above the poverty threshold. For example, if both parents in a married-couple family with two children were employed in EAP-funded jobs paying hourly rates just sufficient to generate a poverty-line income for a family of three, their joint income would be about 56 percent above the poverty line for a family of four. If one parent worked full-time at such a wage, and the other worked half-time, their joint income would be about 17 percent above the poverty threshold for a family of four.

The adoption of such a wage guarantee would, of course, increase the net cost of an EAP jobs program. My estimates of average wage levels in an EAP jobs program are based on the median earnings of employed part-time workers and the average earning capacity of officially unemployed workers. If some members of these groups would have been eligible for EAP wages greater than they could have earned in the private sector, then my estimates are too low.

In addition, if such a wage policy were introduced, some workers employed in the private sector would find it advantageous to abandon their existing private sector jobs in favor of higher-paying EAP positions. The jobs abandoned by these workers would become available to unemployed workers who might otherwise be forced to take EAP-funded jobs, but the program would be left funding higher-paying jobs for low-wage workers with children. At the same time, low-wage workers without children would be drawn into the private sector by increased vacancy rates and by the higher wages that those vacancies might engender.

The possible magnitude of these shifts and their likely impact on wage levels is analyzed in more detail in chapter 4. At this point, I merely want to suggest that such a result can be defended on policy grounds. In addition to ensuring more nearly adequate levels of support for poor children, it would tend to ration low-wage jobs in a socially desirable manner, effectively reserving the lowest-paying positions in the economy for workers without dependent children, while providing low-wage working parents with special help in upgrading their earning capacity.

Given the complexity of these effects, however, estimating the additional cost of paying unskilled working parents an above-market wage would be exceedingly difficult. For this reason, I have not adjusted my estimates to account for the payment of above-market wages to low-wage EAP job-holders with children. It should be noted that this biases my estimate of the program's wage bill in a downward direction, but a large margin for error in that direction is built into my estimate because of the expansive assumptions I have adopted regarding program participation rates.

It is also important to remember that the average wage rates I have assumed an EAP jobs program would have paid are substantially above the level needed to ensure a poverty-line income for even very large families. Even the average wages I have assumed the program would have paid to former AFDC parents would have been sufficient to generate an income above the poverty threshold for the average AFDC family of three. Thus, the negative bias in my estimates attributable to my failure to account for the additional cost of special salary increments for low-wage working parents may not be very significant in absolute terms.

Other Program Costs

The budget of an EAP jobs program would be dominated by its direct wage bill, but there would be other program costs as well. The government would be responsible for the employer's share of social security taxes levied against the program's payroll, and it would presumably be necessary to provide some form of health insurance to program participants. In addition, the program's workforce would have to be provided with physical facilities and equipment, and if single parents were to be employed in significant numbers, provisions for child care would also have to be made. Finally, special rehabilitation and training programs would be needed for large numbers of EAP job candidates, and the program's general administration would have to be funded.

HEALTH INSURANCE

I have assumed that program participants would be offered health insurance equivalent to that made available to existing federal government employees and that it would be offered on the same terms. The most popular such package is a Blue Cross/Blue Shield plan that offers enrollees a choice between two levels of coverage. The "standard option" package provides benefits slightly better than those provided by Medicare, while the "high option" package provides substantially better coverage for a higher employee premium contribution.[16] Between 1977 and 1986, the total annual premium for the standard option plan increased from $127.14 to $688.22 for individual coverage and from 368.68 to $1,659.84 for family coverage. The government paid 75 percent of this premium, and the employee paid the balance. Over the same period, the total annual premium for the high option plan increased from $505.70 to $1,379.04 for individual coverage and from $1,198.86 to $3,017.04 for family coverage, with the government paying between 42 and 53 percent of the premium depending on the year.[17]

I have assumed that all former AFDC parents and all officially unemployed full-time workers with children under eighteen would have elected family coverage, and that the balance of the EAP workforce would have elected individual coverage. I have further assumed that the program's full-time workforce would have chosen the "standard" and "high option" plans in equal numbers, while the program's part-time workers would all have elected to receive the standard plan. In fact, there has been a steady decline over the past decade in the number of federal employees electing the high option as opposed to the low option plan. The high option plan was elected by 83 percent of all enrolled federal employees in 1980, but by 1987 the percentage making that election had declined to 38 percent.[18] Moreover, because of their lower average skill levels, EAP job-holders would have earned wages below the average for other federal employees and would probably have been more likely to elect the lower cost standard option plan.

FACILITIES, TOOLS, AND MATERIALS

In addition to these employee benefits, an EAP jobs program would need physical facilities, tools, and materials to employ its workforce usefully. To accurately estimate these costs is extremely difficult, because their magnitude would vary greatly depending on the types of jobs created by the program and the degree to which the program's workforce was integrated into already-established and equipped government operations.

Some impression of the relative magnitudes involved can be gained by examining the expenditures of the Works Progress Administration (WPA), the largest sustained public employment program established during the 1930s. In table 2.5 I indicate the proportion of all WPA expenditures devoted to non-labor costs by project type. Overall, 25 percent of the program's expenditures were devoted to such costs, but this figure reflected the relative capital intensity of the building and construction projects that provided over three-fourths of all WPA jobs. In the program's smaller community service projects, the proportion of all expenditures devoted to non-labor costs was only about 15 percent.

TABLE 2.5

Proportion of All WPA Expenditures Spent on Nonlabor Costs by Project Type (in percent)

ALL PROJECTS	25.3
Division of Operations	28.1
Highways, Roads, and Streets	29.6
Public Buildings	29.1
Recreational Facilities (except buildings)	23.3
Publicly Owned or Operated Utilities	27.6
Airports and Airways	41.7
Conservation	22.5
Sanitation	23.7
Engineering Surveys	11.8
Division of Community Service Programs	14.9
Public Activities Programs	14.4
Education	16.2
Recreation	17.5
Library	12.9
Museum	10.8
Art	10.6
Music	7.5
Writing	6.9
Research and Records Programs	9.3
Research and Surveys	9.7
Public Records	9.1
Historical Records Surveys	7.7
Welfare Programs	17.9
Public Health and Hospital Work	10.1
Sewing	18.3
Production Projects (except sewing)	13.8
Housekeeping Aides	4.3
Household Workers' Training	15.5
School Lunches	32.4
Distribution of Surplus Commodities	24.3

Source: Arthur E. Burns and Edward A. Williams, *Federal Work, Security and Relief Programs*, Works Progress Administration Monograph 24 (1941, reprint ed., New York: DeCapo Press, 1971), p. 138 (table 7).

Another complicating factor in estimating the materials costs of an EAP jobs program is that procurement expenditures would create additional jobs in the private sector, thereby reducing the number of jobs that the program itself would have to create. About 59 percent of all expenditures for final goods and services in the United States ends up as employee compensation,[19] so approximately this percentage of all EAP materials expenditures could probably be counted as the macroeconomic equivalent of funds spent for EAP employee compensation.

I am not here referring to the possible multiplier effect of EAP spending, since the size of such an effect would depend on the net change in total government expenditures attributable to the establishment of the jobs program. I am merely recognizing that if EAP jobs pay wages equivalent to those earned in the private sector, then every fifteen-thousand-dollar-a-year job created in the private sector to supply materials for the program can be counted as the macroeconomic equivalent of a fifteen-thousand-dollar-a-year EAP job. This means that when adding a sum for materials procurement to an estimate of EAP program costs, it should be possible to subtract almost three-fifths of that amount from the program's estimated employee compensation bill. This would not be possible if instead of guaranteeing work to all job-seekers, the program set out to create a fixed number of jobs. In that case, program expenditures for materials procurement would create the same number of private sector jobs, but it wouldn't reduce the number of positions that the jobs program would have to create.

I have assumed that expenditures for facilities, tools, and materials used in an EAP jobs program would have equaled one-third of the program's total employee compensation costs. This is equivalent to assuming that the program's non-labor costs would have been proportionately as great as those incurred by the WPA. At the same time, I have adjusted my estimate of the program's employee compensation costs downward, in recognition of the additional private sector jobs that the program's non-labor expenditures would have created. However, instead of assuming that these expenditures would have reduced the program's own employee compensation costs by an amount equal to three-fifths of the cost of the materials acquired, I have assumed that the employment "payback" would have been equal to only one-half of the amount of the expenditures, thus allowing for some "leakage" from the employment effect of these expenditures.

CHILD CARE

In estimating total program costs, account also needs to be taken of the child care needs of program participants. It would be unrealistic to expect AFDC parents to take EAP-funded jobs unless affordable child care were made available to them. The challenge posed by this need suggests an interesting possibility. I have not yet discussed the kinds of services that an EAP jobs program could provide for the public, but child care would certainly be a high priority on most lists of unmet community needs, and the ratio of employee salaries to non-labor costs in professional child care operations is within the range assumed for EAP work projects.[20]

What this means is that an EAP jobs program could provide free child care services to its own workforce at no additional program cost. Indeed, the program could provide free child care services to the nation's entire laborforce at no additional program cost. Moreover, the child care service provided could be as labor- and equipment-rich as child care experts thought desirable. Given my projections of the number of positions that an EAP jobs program would need to fund and the assumption I have made that adequate funding for facilities, tools, and materials would also be available, there would be no need to stint in the design of a national child care project. Nor would it matter whether all of the child care facilities were actually operated as part of the EAP jobs program, or whether they directly employed EAP enrollees. Every new job created in the private or regular government sectors would mean one less job that the program itself would have to provide. In other words, funding for child care services could be provided by the jobs program without the program having to operate all of the child care facilities itself (so long as the actual providers were not-for-profit operators who spent all fees for salaries, facilities, and materials).

The value to the community of such an undertaking would be enormous. A study of paid child care in the United States by the Department of Health and Human Services found that government-sponsored slots for full-day child care cost an average of $28.50 a week in 1977, and it found that these costs were rising at approximately the rate of inflation.[21] Expressed in 1986 prices, this amounted to about $51.50 per week or almost $2,700 per child per year.

This data suggests another factor that could affect the cost of an EAP jobs program, namely, the possible willingness of the public to pay part of the cost of EAP work projects out of nonprogram funds. The existence of an EAP jobs program would alter the cost-benefit calculus of providing additional public goods and services in a fundamental way. Desirable services that the public now feels it cannot afford, such as universal publicly-financed child care, could be provided at little or no additional cost to the public. Indeed, as insurance against boondoggleing, it might be desirable to insist that all EAP employment projects provide goods or services for which the public is willing to pay at least part of the cost from nonprogram funds. One way this could be accomplished would be by requiring state or local government sponsorship of EAP work projects to the extent necessary to pay the program's nonlabor costs (with federal assistance being provided where local resources were inadequate). This was the general practice in the New Deal employment programs that most nearly approximated our model.[22]

For example, using the 1977 cost-per-child figures noted above for government-funded child care slots (and assuming that nonlabor costs equaled 25 percent of that total), then the nonlabor cost of providing full-day professional child care equaled only about $7 per child per week, or about $14 per week in current (1989) prices. I do not think it unreasonable to assume that the public would willingly bear that cost, either in the form of additional government spending or in the form of user fees. If EAP-financed community services were partly funded in this way, then the overall cost of an EAP jobs program would be correspondingly less.

ADMINISTRATIVE COSTS AND SPECIAL SERVICES TO PROGRAM PARTICIPANTS

My analysis of the program's ability to provide child care for its workforce applies with equal force to all the other special services that program participants might need—vocational training programs for workers needing to upgrade their skills, special support services for workers with substance-abuse problems, counseling and vocational rehabilitation services for workers with physical or psychological disabilities, sheltered workshop programs for workers unable to cope with the demands of a normal work environment. All these services could be provided at no additional cost to the program, and the same would be true of the program's general administration.

The Bottom Line

The total budgeted cost of an EAP jobs program would therefore consist of just four major items—the program's direct wage bill, the government's share of social security taxes, the government's share of employee health insurance premiums, and an allocation for the facilities, tools, and materials used in the program's work projects. The program's administration would be self-financing. In table 2.6 I provide a summary of these costs for the ten-year period under consideration. The estimates range from a low of $66.1 billion in 1978 to a high of $175.3 billion in 1983.

The net cost of such a program would have been less than this, however, because the government would have immediately recouped a portion of the program's budgeted cost in the form of increased tax revenues. This is because wages paid to program participants would be taxable income, unlike the cash and in-kind benefits that the wages would replace. Taxable income is now generated, of course, when cash assistance payments are spent by transfer payment beneficiaries or when the government makes vendor payments on their behalf. The difference is that EAP wages would also be taxable income to the immediate recipient of those wages. Thus, the payment of wages by an EAP jobs program would result

44

TABLE 2.6
Estimated Cost of an EAP Jobs Program: 1977 to 1986 (in billions)

	1977	1978	1979	1980	1981	1982	1983	1984	1985	1986	10-Year Total
Budgeted Cost	70.4	66.1	69.8	98.3	117.1	161.5	175.3	144.0	142.2	142.5	1,187.2
Wages	49.2	46.1	48.7	68.3	80.9	111.1	119.3	97.1	95.8	96.5	813.0
Benefits	4.8	4.6	4.9	7.2	9.2	13.4	16.2	14.5	14.4	13.8	103.0
Materials	16.4	15.4	16.2	22.8	27.0	37.0	39.8	32.4	32.0	32.2	271.2
Tax Savings	14.0	13.1	13.9	19.9	24.6	33.8	36.3	29.9	30.0	30.4	245.9
Net Cost	56.4	53.0	55.9	78.4	92.5	127.7	139.0	114.1	112.2	112.1	941.3

Sources and Assumptions: See Appendix.

in an "extra" round of income tax collections when compared to existing income maintenance programs.

In addition, government expenditures for the facilities, tools, and supplies used in the program would also create additional taxable income. Once again, I am not here referring to the general multiplier effect that EAP spending might have, but merely to the additional taxable income that would be immediately attributable to program expenditures. In the case of the program's direct wage bill, the linkage is obvious. In the case of program expenditures for facilities, tools, and supplies, the additional taxable income would consist of the wages, rent, interest, and profits that the government purchases would generate in the private sector.

Estimates of the funds that would be recouped as a result of these additional tax payments are included in table 2.6, with a resulting estimate of the program's net cost. This estimate varies from a low of $53 billion in 1978 to a high of $139 billion in 1983. It is estimated that for the entire ten-year period, the program's net cost would have been $941.3 billion. This is a great deal of money, but only about half as much as was spent on the nation's core Social Security programs during the same period.[23]

It would be interesting to ask the American public whether it would have accepted a 50 percent increase in Social Security taxes between 1977 and 1986 in exchange for a statutory right to employment at market wages in a public sector job. In 1986 this would have meant a 3.6 point increase in Social Security tax rates for both employers and employees (from 7.15 percent to 10.75 percent). My guess is that employment security is sufficiently valued by American workers and their families that such an offer would have received overwhelming public support if it were fairly presented.

In fact, however, it would not have required this large a tax increase to fund an EAP jobs program. A significant portion of the program's net cost would have been covered by reduced expenditures for the nation's existing income transfer programs. It is now time to estimate the size of these savings.

SAVINGS IN OTHER PROGRAMS

In table 2.7 I provide a summary of the means-tested antipoverty benefits provided by all levels of government in the United States between
1977 and 1986. Unemployment Insurance (UI), and Social Security (OAS-
DHI) benefit payments have not been included in the table because eligibility for those benefits is not subject to a means test. It should be
noted, however, that because of the way in which they are financed and
the nature of the populations they serve, both UI and OASDHI have a
significant antipoverty effect in practice.

The table shows that the total amount spent providing antipoverty benefits increased from $74.8 billion in 1978 to $145.9 billion in 1986. Ad-
justing the figures for inflation, the real level of expenditures is shown to
have been much more stable, ranging from a low of $134.6 billion in 1982
to a high of $145.9 billion in 1986, expressed in constant (1986) dollars.
Given the overall growth in government expenditures that occurred during the period, this relative stability in antipoverty spending meant that
a declining share of the nation's public resources were being devoted to
antipoverty efforts. The share of all government spending (federal, state,
and local) devoted to the antipoverty programs listed in table 2.7 declined from 11 percent in 1977 to 8.9 percent in 1985.[24] Real spending
per person living in poverty declined 18 percent between 1977 and 1986.
If expenditures for medical care are excluded, the decline was 24 percent.

In fact, the decline in spending within the period was greater than
these figures suggest. Real antipoverty expenditures per person living in
poverty actually rose slightly from 1977 to 1978, but in the next four years
they plummeted almost 31 percent. Between 1982 and 1986, only about
one-third of this loss was recouped. If expenditures for medical care are
excluded, the decline in antipoverty spending per person living in poverty was over 35 percent between 1978 and 1982, with only 22 percent
of this loss being recouped by 1986.[25] However the decline is measured,
the point that needs to be emphasized is that the period in question was
one in which large cuts in government spending for antipoverty programs
were absorbed relative both to the public's ability to pay for such aid and
to the number of people needing it.

Only a portion of the funds listed in table 2.7 would have been available for reallocation to an EAP jobs program under the terms of the proposal being considered. Only those benefits provided to able-bodied persons of working age and their dependents would have been eliminated.
All benefits provided to (1) persons sixty-five years of age and older, (2)
disabled persons, and (3) children lacking the support of both their parents would remain unchanged.

TABLE 2.7
Summary of Antipoverty Benefits Provided by All Levels of Government: 1977 to 1986 (in billions)

	1977	1978	1979	1980	1981	1982	1983	1984	1985	1986	10-Year Total
Total Spending											
Current Dollars	74.8	82.4	90.6	103.0	117.8	118.5	126.9	133.1	140.6	145.9	1,134.0
1986 Dollars	135.3	138.5	136.9	137.1	142.0	134.6	139.7	140.5	143.3	145.9	1,393.8
Medical Care	22.9	23.7	26.9	31.7	38.8	40.0	43.4	44.5	48.3	51.9	372.1
Medicaid	17.3	18.9	21.8	25.8	30.4	32.4	35.0	37.6	41.2	44.7	305.1
Other	5.6	4.8	5.1	5.9	8.4	7.6	8.4	6.9	7.1	7.2	67.0
Cash Aid	24.3	24.7	25.7	29.4	32.6	33.3	34.7	36.6	38.1	40.8	320.2
AFDC	11.5	11.8	12.0	13.4	14.6	14.6	15.4	16.1	16.7	17.8	143.9
SSI	6.8	7.1	7.5	8.4	9.3	9.8	10.1	11.2	11.9	12.8	94.9
Other	6.0	5.8	6.2	7.6	8.7	8.9	9.2	9.3	9.5	10.2	81.4
Food Aid	8.7	9.4	11.2	14.1	16.2	16.3	18.6	19.7	20.1	20.1	154.4
Food Stamps	5.7	5.9	7.3	9.6	11.8	11.7	13.3	13.3	13.5	13.5	105.6
Other	3.0	3.5	3.9	4.5	4.4	4.6	5.3	6.4	6.6	6.6	48.8
Housing and Energy Aid	6.2	7.6	8.9	10.5	12.9	13.8	14.5	15.0	16.4	15.4	121.6
Education Aid	4.0	3.5	4.6	4.6	4.9	7.9	8.0	8.3	10.1	10.6	66.5
Jobs and Training	5.5	9.8	9.3	8.7	7.6	4.1	4.2	5.5	4.0	3.7	62.4
Social Services	3.2	3.7	4.0	4.0	4.8	3.1	3.5	3.5	3.6	3.4	36.8

Source: U.S. Library of Congress, Congressional Research Office, Cash and Non-Cash Benefits for Persons with Limited Income: Eligibility Rules, Recipient and Expenditure Data (annual).

TABLE 2.8

Estimate of Cash and Noncash Expenditures for Income Maintenance Benefits Provided to Low-Income Families with Able-Bodied Heads under Age 65: 1977 to 1986 (in billions)

	1977	1978	1979	1980	1981	1982	1983	1984	1985	1986	10-Year Total
Total Spending											
Current Dollars	52.0	55.4	57.7	69.0	76.0	78.0	90.4	81.9	80.6	83.5	724.5
1986 Dollars	94.1	93.1	87.2	91.8	91.6	88.6	99.5	86.5	82.2	83.5	898.1
Cash Aid	26.7	23.8	23.5	30.8	34.2	39.8	48.7	36.7	35.3	38.1	337.6
UI	14.1	11.1	10.7	15.6	17.6	23.3	31.3	18.7	16.9	18.2	177.5
AFDC	10.5	10.8	11.0	12.2	13.3	13.3	14.1	14.7	15.2	16.2	131.3
Other	2.1	1.9	1.8	3.0	3.3	3.2	3.3	3.3	3.2	3.7	28.8
Medical Care	7.0	7.3	7.7	9.1	10.3	10.1	10.9	11.2	12.0	13.0	98.6
Medicaid	6.3	6.6	7.0	8.3	8.9	9.1	9.8	10.1	10.9	11.9	88.9
Other	0.7	0.7	0.7	0.8	1.4	1.0	1.1	1.1	1.1	1.1	9.7
Food Aid	7.3	7.9	9.5	11.8	13.6	13.7	15.7	16.6	17.0	17.0	130.1
Food Stamps	4.8	5.0	6.2	8.1	10.0	9.9	11.3	11.3	11.5	11.5	89.6
Other	2.5	2.9	3.3	3.7	3.6	3.8	4.4	5.3	5.5	5.5	40.5
Housing and Energy Aid	3.6	4.4	5.2	6.1	7.5	8.0	8.5	8.7	9.6	9.0	70.6
Jobs and Training	5.5	9.8	9.3	8.7	7.6	4.1	4.2	5.5	4.0	3.7	62.4
Education Aid	1.0	1.2	1.4	1.4	1.5	1.6	1.6	1.8	1.9	1.9	15.3
Social Services	0.9	1.0	1.1	1.1	1.3	0.7	0.8	1.4	0.8	0.8	9.9

Sources and Assumptions: See Appendix.

Unfortunately, the data necessary to determine exactly what share of the benefits listed in table 2.7 went to such persons are not readily available. In some instances the nature of a program allows for an easy categorization of its beneficiaries. Such is the case, for example, with the Supplemental Security Income program (SSI). It pays benefits only to elderly, blind, or totally disabled persons. In other cases, the division of benefits between the families of able-bodied persons of working age and other recipients can be estimated with a fair degree of precision from published data. This is true of the Medicaid program. There are a number of programs, however, for which only rough estimates of the division can be made, based on very limited data. In these cases I have tried to adopt conservative assumptions regarding the proportion of all benefit payments going to able-bodied persons, so that the error in the estimates would be more likely to result in an understatement than in an overstatement of the funds available for reallocation to an EAP jobs program.

In table 2.8 I show the results of these calculations. It provides a rough but conservative estimate of all income maintenance benefits provided to able-bodied persons of working age and their dependents between 1977 and 1986. Recalling that, for purposes of simplification, I am assuming that Unemployment Insurance would also be supplanted by the jobs program, all UI expenditures have also been included in the table. Thus, table 2.8 provides an estimate of all the funds that would have been available for reallocation to an EAP jobs program during the ten-year period in question.

According to this estimate, the amount of aid distributed to able-bodied persons and their families totaled $724.5 billion over the ten-year period. Expressed in constant (1986) dollars, aid levels varied from a high of $99.5 billion in 1983 to a low of $82.2 billion in 1985. As with antipoverty assistance in general, though, these figures are more meaningful if they are measured against the size of the population that needed such assistance. If official unemployment figures are treated as an index of the total number of persons needing the kind of public assistance listed in table 2.8, then the amount of aid provided such persons declined by 25 percent from 1977 to 1986.

Once again as with antipoverty assistance in general these ten-year figures understate the dramatic decline that occurred in the provision of public assistance to the unemployed between 1978, when the unemployment rate averaged 6.0 percent, and 1982, when the unemployment rate averaged 9.5 percent. During this four-year period the amount of aid provided per unemployed person declined 45 percent, and only 27 percent of this loss was recouped over the next four years.[26]

The decline that occurred in antipoverty spending generally during the ten-year period under consideration, and particularly in antipoverty spending for the unemployed, has important implications for my analysis. This is because it significantly diminished the size of the pool of funds that I am assuming would have been available to fund an EAP jobs program. If the relative share of all government spending allocated to income maintenance benefits for able-bodied persons of working age had remained at the 1977 level for the entire ten-year period, then the amount of money available for reallocation to an EAP jobs program would have equaled about $881 billion instead of the $725 billion I have estimated.

Table 2.9 contains a summary report of my estimates of both the annual net cost of an EAP jobs program and of the annual savings that would have been realized from cutbacks in other benefit programs consequent upon the implementation of a policy of providing employment assurance. It is estimated that once allowance is made for these savings, the ten-year funding shortfall for an EAP jobs program would have equaled $217.8 billion. The table also provides an estimate of what the program's funding deficit would have been if the relative share of all government spending allocated for the support of able-bodied persons of working age had remained at the 1977 level for the entire period. It is estimated that if 1977 spending patterns had been maintained, the program's ten-year funding deficit would have totaled only $60.2 billion, with the whole of that amount attributable to the 1982 and 1983 recession years.

TABLE 2.9
Estimate of Additional Funding Needed to Finance an EAP Jobs Program: 1977 to 1986 (in billions)

	1977	1978	1979	1980	1981	1982	1983	1984	1985	1986	10-Year Total
Net Cost of EAP Jobs Program	56.4	53.0	55.9	78.4	92.5	127.7	139.0	114.1	112.2	112.1	941.3
Savings from Cutbacks in Other Programs	52.0	55.4	57.7	69.0	76.0	78.0	90.4	81.9	80.6	83.5	724.5
Funding Surplus or Deficit	−4.4	1.4	1.8	−9.4	−16.5	−49.7	−48.6	−32.2	−31.6	−28.6	−217.8
Funding Surplus or Deficit if 1977 Spending Pattern Had Been Maintained	−4.4	3.8	7.5	−5.3	−7.9	−33.7	−36.0	−5.2	8.3	12.7	−60.2

Sources and Assumptions: See Appendix.

A \$217.8 billion deficit would have amounted to less than 2 percent of all government tax receipts for the period. If financed entirely by higher social security taxes, an increase in Social Security tax rates of about 12 percent would have been required to cover the deficit. In 1986, for example, an increase in both employer and employee contribution rates from 7.15 percent to about 8.05 percent would have been required. If the ten-year deficit had been \$60.2 billion, then the required increase in contribution rates would have been only about 3.5 percent, equivalent to an increase in the 1986 contribution rate from 7.15 percent to about 7.4 percent.[27]

Moreover, these estimates do not take into consideration the possibility, mentioned in my discussion of child care, that the public would willingly bear part of the cost of an EAP jobs program (in the form of additional local taxes or user fees) to obtain the services the program would provide. If, for example, all purchases of equipment and materials for an EAP jobs program were financed in this way, then savings from cutbacks in other programs would have exceeded the net cost of the jobs program by over \$50 billion over the ten-year period.

This result is encouraging. Further study is needed regarding the likely cost of an EAP jobs program and of the likely savings it would generate, but my preliminary analysis suggests that such a program is easily within our fiscal grasp. The provision of employment assurance is an affordable alternative to existing methods of channeling public assistance to able-bodied persons of working age. There are a range of questions regarding the desirability of such a policy that must still be explored, but the idea cannot be dismissed as fiscally utopian.

Combating Unemployment and Poverty

No POLICY response to the problem of unemployment is free of draw-backs. In assessing the effectiveness and desirability of an EAP jobs pro-gram, it is therefore important to remember the costs that unemploy-ment itself imposes on society. The question that has to be answered is not whether a policy of providing employment assurance by means of deliberate public sector hiring would be free of negative side effects. It is whether the shortcomings of such a policy would be as severe as those associated with the existing policy regime.

In other words, we need to consider not only whether an EAP job would satisfy all the economic, social, and psychological needs of unem-ployed persons, but whether those needs are better met by involuntary idleness accompanied by limited income transfers. We need to consider not only whether there would be problematic economic side effects at-tributable to an EAP jobs program, but whether those side effects would be worse than those attributable to continuing high levels of unemploy-ment and its attendant poverty. We need to consider not only the for-midable administrative problems associated with the operation of an EAP jobs program, but whether those problems are greater than those that would have to be overcome to make existing programs and policies work equally well in combating the effects of unemployment and poverty. In short, the issue that needs to be addressed is not whether an EAP jobs program would provide an ideal solution to the nation's unemployment problem, but whether it would constitute a better response to that prob-lem than existing policies.

Before beginning my analysis of the effectiveness of an EAP jobs pro-gram, I therefore want briefly to review the social costs attributable to unemployment under existing conditions. These costs can be roughly cat-egorized under three headings. The first consists of the income mainte-nance benefits that society must provide for people because they cannot support themselves. An estimate of the size of these expenditures in the United States was reported in table 2.8 above. Expressed in constant (1986) dollars, they averaged almost $90 billion a year between 1977 and 1986, costing the average American household over a thousand dollars per year.

Society pays for unemployment a second time, though, by forfeiting the additional goods and services that would be produced if everyone

who wanted a job was productively employed. In table 2.6 I provided a rough estimate of the additional domestic production sacrificed in the United States between 1977 and 1986 because of our failure to provide work for the nation's entire laborforce. This lost production totaled almost $1.2 trillion. Expressed in constant (1986) dollars, it amounted to about $142 billion annually, a sacrifice of approximately $1,600 dollars worth of goods and services per household each year.

What is particularly disheartening about this sacrifice is its seeming irrationality. In table 2.8 I showed that we actually spent most of what it would have cost to obtain these additional goods and services. We simply chose to support the unemployed in forced idlesness rather than provide them with useful work. Economists are fond of pointing out that there is no such thing as a free lunch, but the increased production that the United States would enjoy if it used its resources to employ productively everyone who wants to work, is a lunch for which we are already paying close to the full price.

Finally, society pays for unemployment a third time with the private suffering and public insecurity it causes. We pay for it with broken homes, with child and spouse abuse, with mental and physical illness, with crime, and with a host of other social problems. Of course none of these ills can be laid entirely, or even primarily, at the feet of the nation's unemployment problem, but can anyone doubt that unemployment makes them worse? It has been noted, for example, that arrest rates among youths employed in the federally funded summer jobs program decline by over 50 percent while they are employed. The resultant savings in reduced criminal justice system costs, and in reduced property and personal injury losses, were estimated to average $1,150 per participant in the late 1970s.[1]

Another study has estimated that the increase in the U.S. unemployment rate that occurred between 1973 and 1974 resulted in a 2.3 percent increase in total mortality, a 2.8 percent increase in deaths due to cardiovascular disease, a 1.4 percent increase in cirrhosis mortality, a 6.0 percent increase in mental hospital admissions, a 6.0 percent increase in the overall arrest rate, a 1.1 percent increase in assaults, and a 1.0 percent increase in suicide.[2] The methodology that produced these estimates has been criticized, so the actual numbers may not be reliable, but few authorities doubt the existence of at least some causal association between unemployment and the major indicators of medical and social pathology.[3]

The social costs of unemployment are substantial, and my estimates of the net funding requirements of an EAP jobs program account for only some of them. Specifically, I have counted the cost of providing income transfers to employable persons, but my estimates do not take into consideration either the opportunity costs of foregone production that soci-

ety incurs because of involuntary unemployment, or the positive costs of the medical, psychological, and social problem that unemployment generates or aggravates. Ideally, account should be taken of all of these factors in estimating the real net cost of an EAP jobs program.

Since I have not tried to do this, it is particularly important to keep the social costs of unemployment in mind when discussing the limitations and negative side effects of an EAP jobs program. The program would have to impose costs on society greater than these for it to be deemed inferior to existing policies.

In the balance of this chapter I analyze the effectiveness of an EAP jobs program as a policy response to the distinct problems posed by frictional, cyclical, and structural unemployment, and I then conclude with a brief assessment of the program's overall effectiveness as an antipoverty measure. In chapter 4 I analyze the likely economic side effects of such a program, and in chapter 5 I consider the administrative problems and opportunities it would present.

FRICTIONAL UNEMPLOYMENT

Frictional unemployment results from the economy's inefficient handling of economically beneficial behavior. A willingness on the part of workers to move from less to more productive jobs is good for both the economy and individual workers. It is not desirable, however, for the transition to include a period of involuntary unemployment. Society loses production and frictionally unemployed workers lose income.

The existence of significant frictional unemployment may also affect job-switching behavior in undesirable ways. The prospect of having to submit to a period of involuntary unemployment while seeking a new job may inhibit workers from voluntarily leaving their present jobs, even when a change in employment is desired. Also, the pressures of being unemployed are likely to induce a short, albeit intense job search effort. Where information about available jobs is difficult and time-consuming to obtain, this kind of search effort may not be optimal.

For these reasons, a reduction in the rate of frictional unemployment is desirable, but how can it be achieved? The primary determinant of the rate of frictional unemployment is the efficiency of information flows between job-seekers and employers. In a world of perfect information, there would be no frictional unemployment. Workers would move quickly and costlessly to the best job open to them. Thus, any improvement in the efficiency of the process whereby job-seekers and potential employers learn about one another will tend to reduce the rate of frictional unemployment. Frictional unemployment cannot be entirely eliminated, but a minimization of the rate can and should be an objective of public policy.

Would an EAP jobs program have any effect on the rate of frictional unemployment? The existence of such a program would probably make workers more willing voluntarily to abandon their current jobs, because they would know that "fall-back" employment was guaranteed. By itself, this would tend to increase the rate of frictional unemployment (though the increase might be disguised in the form of increased EAP participation rates). As noted above, however, an increased willingness on the part of workers to move from less to more productive jobs is desirable in itself. The goal of public policy in this area should not be to discourage job-switching behavior, but to improve the efficiency of the matching of available workers and jobs.

Would an EAP jobs program affect the efficiency of the job matching process? The efficiency of the process is a function of three factors: the cost and intensity of the recruiting efforts of employers, the cost and intensity of the job search efforts of workers, and the quality of the institutional mechanisms that facilitate the flow of information between job-seekers and employers. An EAP jobs program would influence each of these factors, but in different directions, so the net effect of the program on the rate of frictional unemployment is theoretically indeterminate.

Employer job recruiting efforts would tend to increase with the achievement of effective full employment because of the increased difficulty of finding and attracting qualified job applicants. Waiting for job applicants to appear at the door is a luxury that employers can enjoy only when unemployment rates are high.

The effect of an EAP jobs program on the job-seeking behavior of employees is less clear. The availability of guaranteed jobs would probably tend to reduce the intensity of job search efforts by unemployed workers, while the elimination of existing income maintenance benefits for unemployed workers would have the opposite effect. It is unclear which tendency would predominate. The degree to which the job-seeking behavior of unemployed workers is affected by transfer programs like UI is a much debated question,[4] and the tendency for workers to reduce their job search efforts because of the availability of EAP jobs might be counteracted by the increased willingness of workers to risk a job change. In short, the net effect of an EAP jobs program on employee job search behavior is far from certain.

Finally, the establishment of an EAP jobs program would probably facilitate the development of more effective institutional mechanisms for transferring information between employers and job-seekers. Increased job recruiting efforts by employers would encourage both an expansion and rationalization of the activities of private employment services, and state-operated employment services might experience a similar revival. There is substantial room for improvement in the effectiveness of state employment services,[5] but the necessary political impetus has been lacking for a rationalization of the system. The establishment of an EAP jobs program could change that by strengthening political interest in such reforms. Under current conditions, most employers have little interest in the effectiveness of state employment services because they do not need them to locate job applicants. With a tightening of the labor market, however, employers would have a strong incentive to support a strengthening of the state system, if only to shift their increased job recruiting costs onto the government. A "window" of political opportunity for significant reform in this area could therefore emerge.

An EAP jobs program would also contribute to the efficiency of state employment services in more direct ways. The program would serve as an efficient viaduct for conveying information about job openings in the regular labor market to unemployed workers, and the employment records of participants in the program would provide a valuable source of information for potential employers.

So far, the cost of these behavioral and institutional changes hasn't been mentioned. My analysis of their character, though, suggests that one major effect of an EAP jobs program would be to shift job search costs from employees to employers. Employers would be forced to spend more on job recruitment, while the costs of job search efforts by workers would tend to diminish. This latter tendency would arise both because employers would be making greater efforts to reach potential job applicants and because information-transmitting institutions would probably become more efficient.

This shift in the burden of job search costs should probably be regarded as desirable. Unless one believes that unemployment is caused by a lack of initiative on the part of unemployed workers, it is arguably both unjust and inefficient to require them to bear the primary burden of society's job-matching costs. It is unjust because it forces the innocent victims of a social problem to bear a disproportionate share of its costs. It is inefficient because employers are generally in a better position than unemployed workers to improve the flow of information necessary to reduce the rate of frictional unemployment. If employers bore a greater share of society's job-matching costs, they would have an incentive to devise more efficient means of accomplishing the task.

There is one final issue that needs to be addressed in reference to the likely effect of an EAP jobs program on frictional unemployment. In my earlier comments concerning the program's probable impact on the job search behavior of workers, I mentioned in passing that the effect of existing income maintenance programs on such behavior is a matter of some controversy. This debate largely concerns the effect of programs like UI on the reservation wage of job-seekers (the minimum wage offer that will induce them to accept employment). The argument advanced by critics of these programs is that the wage expectations of unemployed workers tend to be too high because of the substantial opportunity costs that the forfeiture of income transfers places on the acceptance of low-wage employment. Thus, it may not be the effect of an EAP jobs program on job search intensity that would concern critics of traditional income maintenance programs so much as its effect on reservation wages. This is an important issue, but I shall defer discussion of it until chapter 4.

What conclusions can be drawn, then, from this discussion of frictional unemployment? First, the net effect of an EAP jobs program on the rate of frictional unemployment is uncertain, even as to its direction. Second, job recruitment efforts and their costs would almost certainly increase for employers. Third, the program's effect on job search behavior by workers is uncertain. Fourth, some improvement in the quality of information-transmitting institutions operating in the labor market could be antici-pated. Finally, the aggregate cost of society's job-matching efforts would tend to shift from workers to employers.

CYCLICAL UNEMPLOYMENT

In discussing the impact of an EAP jobs program on cyclical unemploy-ment, it is useful to distinguish between the program's anticyclical ten-dencies and its effectiveness in meeting the needs of cyclically unem-ployed workers. I shall consider each of these factors in turn.

I have already noted that an EAP jobs program would be a powerful automatic stabilizer. It would function much like UI in this respect, but its impact would be greater due to its broader coverage and to the fact that it would replace a greater proportion of the lost income of cyclically unemployed workers. In addition, an EAP jobs program would probably affect discretionary anticyclical policy in a beneficial way. The existence of a free-standing employment assurance program would free policymak-ing in this area from excessive concern for the near-term employment effects of particular anticyclical strategies. Both macro and microeco-nomic policy could assume a longer-term focus, and political debate regarding adopted policies would be less hobbled by acrimonious dis-agreements over the amount of "pain" caused by a particular policy's short-term effect on employment levels.

The same salutary effect would probably be felt in the execution of anticyclical policy as well. Because of the exceptionally strong political pressures that develop during recessions, it is difficult to maintain a par-ticular anticyclical policy long enough properly to judge its effects. Unless immediate improvements in the economy's performance are evident, political pressure quickly mounts to try something else, whether or not a change in policy seems warranted on theoretical grounds. Stability in the execution of anticyclical policy would be easier to achieve if those who must bear its short-term burdens were more adequately compensated.

Moreover, with such compensation provided automatically by an EAP jobs program, policy choices might reflect a better balancing of competing interests in society. The long-term effects of recessions are not uniformly negative, and although few policymakers will openly admit it, they frequently do favor policies that are procyclical, usually with the stated purpose of fighting inflation. The tight monetary policy adopted by the Federal Reserve Board in the 1980–82 period provides the clearest example of such a strategy. By more effectively compensating those harmed by such policies, an EAP jobs program could reduce the resistance of short-term losers to policies that really do promise net long-term gains. Also, policymakers representing the interests of those likely to gain from a procyclical policy would be induced to take fuller account of the social costs of the policies they favor. Those policies would have a "price tag" attached in the form of increased EAP expenditures.

This last point warrants special emphasis. Only if the gainers from a proposed public policy initiative are forced to compensate the losers can we be relatively certain that policy decisions will tend to increase aggregate social welfare. Even in a plus-sum game a majority of the players may be losers, and it is by no means clear that such a game increases aggregate social welfare. More to the point, even if a majority of the players do gain, the losses endured by the minority may be so severe and socially destructive that the game diminishes net social welfare. If side bets by nonparticipants are taxed to increase the size of the pot, then Russian roulette is, in monetary terms, a plus-sum game in which all players but one win. It would be hard to argue, though, that such a game increases the aggregate social welfare of the players. This is because losers forfeit more than money. The same is true of unemployment.

Given a commitment to compensate the victims of cyclical unemployment, how well would an EAP jobs program serve that end in comparison with existing income transfer programs? The principal needs of cyclically unemployed workers are threefold. First, they need income to replace their lost wages. Second, they need to maintain the nonspecific work habits that link them to the laborforce and to either conserve the specific skills that define their occupation or learn new skills. Third, they need assistance in dealing with the personal problems (psychological, medical, and familial) that unemployment either causes or aggravates.

Given the nature of these needs, it hardly seems necessary to argue that most cyclically unemployed workers would be better served by an

offer of work in an EAP jobs program than by existing income maintenance programs. A higher proportion of lost income would be replaced.
Nonspecific work habits and skills would be maintained by continued
work rather than eroded by a period of forced idleness. Many specialized
skills could continue to be practiced and new skills could be learned.
Finally, the best antidote for the traumatizing effects of unemployment
is a good job paying decent wages. An EAP jobs program could provide
that antidote. Only those workers who are assured of a relatively quick
recall to their former jobs are likely to be better served by the provision
of income maintenance benefits like UI.

Whether an EAP jobs program would serve the interests of employers
is less certain. Industries that employ cyclically unemployed workers
during periods of economic expansion clearly have an interest in the
maintenance of the skill levels of cyclically unemployed workers, as they
have in the maintenance of their mental and physical well-being. On the
other hand, it is by no means clear that employers have an interest in
having the lost wages of cyclically unemployed workers replaced or in
having such workers find alternative employment. The anticyclical effect
of replacing lost wages is consistent with employer interests in economic
recovery, but employers are also interested in strengthening their bargaining position with labor and in the ready availability of cyclically unemployed workers for reemployment when their services are needed.
Both of these interests are better served by the maintenance of cyclically
unemployed workers in a state of idleness and relative impoverishment.

Whether employer interests correspond to the public interest in this
regard is another matter. I shall defer consideration of the general effects
of a shift in bargaining power from employers to workers until chapter 4.
At this point I shall limit my discussion to the issue of whether an EAP
jobs program would discourage the reentry of cyclically unemployed
workers into the regular laborforce following a recession.

The program's likely effect on the willingness of cyclically unemployed
workers to accept reemployment in the private sector following a recession would depend on the relative attractiveness of EAP jobs in comparison with those available through the regular labor market. This is also an
issue, of course, under the current policy regime. Indeed, the problem
is inherently more troublesome under existing conditions. Cyclically unemployed workers now face a choice between more vigorous job-seeking
behavior (to regain their old jobs or to find substitute employment) and
continued reliance on any income maintenance benefits for which they
may be eligible while unemployed. Essentially, this is a choice between
income-without-work and a job. To ensure adequate job-seeking behavior under these circumstances, it is necessary to require unemployed
workers to furnish proof of their job search activities as a condition for

the receipt of income maintenance benefits and to keep those benefits well below prevailing wage levels.[6]

If cyclically unemployed workers faced a choice between two jobs, instead of between income-without-work and a job, this kind of coercion would not be necessary. Even marginal differences in wages or working conditions should induce EAP job-holders to accept employment offers in the private sector. So long as an EAP jobs program did not engage in a bidding war to keep its workforce from accepting such offers, private sector employers should have little difficulty in hiring workers away from the program, though they might have to increase their wage offers to do so.

It would also be possible to impose a requirement that program participants be ready and willing to accept suitable private sector employment. Such a requirement would probably meet little resistance among program participants, so long as "suitable employment" was not defined to include jobs that were significantly less attractive than those provided by the jobs program. This should pose no problem. The assumption made throughout this analysis is that an EAP jobs program would offer employment on terms approximating those available to similarly qualified workers in the regular labor market. This means that resistance to reemployment in the regular labor market would arise only if program participants were pressured to accept private sector jobs paying lower wages or offering poorer working conditions than those generally available to workers with similar qualifications and work histories.

STRUCTURAL UNEMPLOYMENT

The concept of structural unemployment is frequently evoked to explain the joblessness of minority youths who are handicapped by a lack of marketable skills, little prior employment experience, and residence in communities with few employment opportunities. Properly speaking, though, the term encompasses the personal histories of broadly disparate groups—rural workers left stranded by changes in the agricultural sector, workers in manufacturing industries that have undergone significant technological or organizational transformations or that have moved to "greener pastures," workers in industries that are dying as a result of changes in consumer tastes or international competition, and older women workers who have difficulty entering or reentering the labor market after raising a family. The term also properly encompasses unemployment attributable to bulges in the age distribution of the population, to a diminution in the long-term rate of economic growth, or to any number of other causes.

In short, structural unemployment is an analytical basket category. To say that unemployment in a particular population group is caused by a change in the structure of the economy tells us nothing more than that the demand for the group's labor, or the supply of it available for employment, has shifted for reasons that cannot be characterized as frictional or cyclical. The cause of the shift may be technological, demographic, behavioral, ecological, or something else entirely.

The underlying cause of a particular type of structural unemployment may be either good or bad for the economy as a whole. Whether the underlying trend is beneficial or harmful, however, its immediate effect on workers left unemployed is clearly negative. As with policies that cause or prolong cyclical unemployment, society imposes a disproportionate share of the social cost of these adjustments on individuals who have little control over the decisions that necessitate them. Equitable considerations suggest that persons enduring personal hardship for the sake of the common good should be compensated by society for the harm they suffer.

The specific needs of structurally unemployed workers are as diverse as the causes of their unemployment. For purposes of general policy analysis, though, they can be categorized under two headings. The first encompasses needs that arise because of the existence of geographic or occupational disequilibria in the labor market, that is, where jobs requiring the skills possessed by unemployed workers are not available in the communities where they live, but jobs for which they would qualify are available elsewhere, or jobs are available locally for workers possessing different qualifications.

The second category of needs associated with structural unemployment are those attributable to quantitative disequilibria in the labor market that would not be corrected either by retraining or increased geographic mobility. There is no reason why a structural change in the economy must necessarily create as many jobs as it eliminates.[7] If the number of newly created jobs is inadequate to employ all of the workers rendered redundant by structural changes in the economy, or if not enough new jobs are being created to provide work for all new entrants to the labor force, then a structurally unemployed work force may come into existence for which neither geographic mobility nor job training alone will provide relief.

Because structural unemployment manifests itself in these two ways, a two-pronged strategy is needed to meet the needs of structurally unemployed workers. First, efforts are needed to better equip or situate structurally unemployed workers to let them compete for available jobs. Second, additional jobs are needed to fill any remaining employment deficit. An EAP jobs program would be well suited to achieve both of these goals.

Any amount of job training could be built into an EAP jobs program without increasing its net cost. Each position created for either a trainer or a trainee is one less job the program would otherwise have to create. Indeed, a high quality training program could probably be operated at a lower cost per position than other work projects, since persons enrolled in such a program would probably be willing to accept a reduced stipend as compared to regular EAP jobs.

Significant improvements could also be expected in the coordination of government-sponsored job training activities with private sector needs. The existence of a tight labor market would probably generate greater interest on the part of private employers in supporting government-sponsored job training programs, and state employment services would be well situated to play a coordinating role. Information collected by state employment services about the qualifications of EAP participants and about the laborforce needs of local employers would provide an excellent source of data for improved human resource planning.

Geographic disequilibria in the labor market could also be identified and appropriate remedial steps could be fashioned. This might involve nothing more than providing specific information to employers and job-seekers about the availability of jobs or appropriately qualified unemployed workers in other communities or regions. With computerized access to a regional or national data base, this service could be quick, cheap, and personal. In circumstances where it would be desirable to encourage workers to relocate, relocation assistance could be provided.

Regulating access to training programs in an EAP jobs program would also provide an excellent means of maintaining discipline and morale among program participants. This could be especially important for youthful EAP participants, many of whom would have little prior employment experience and few marketable job skills. For such persons, placement in a training program could be conditioned on first establishing a satisfactory performance record in an unskilled EAP job. Nor would such a requirement function only as a discipline and morale-boosting device. For young workers with little prior employment experience, the development of good general work habits is one of the first goals of an individualized job training program. Working in an "entry level" EAP job seems an appropriate means of cultivating those habits. For this reason, it is a logical preliminary to more specific skill training. Even formal educational programs would receive indirect support from an EAP jobs program, since it could effectively serve as a greatly expanded work-study program for both secondary and postsecondary students.

Finally, it is worth noting that an EAP jobs program could also serve as a vehicle for the establishment of vocational rehabilitation programs and sheltered workshops for handicapped or partially disabled workers. Whether the workshops provided permanent jobs or served as training facilities, they would confer substantial benefits on both society and the individuals served.[8]

As I have noted, structural unemployment may involve a net job deficit as well as skill or geographic disequilibria in the labor market. It is in responding to this problem that an EAP jobs program could perhaps do the most good of all. For example, a bulge in the age distribution of a population may tax an economy's ability to create sufficient employment opportunities to meet a rapidly growing supply of workers. The difficulty may persist for years or even decades. What young workers need in such circumstances is not simply job training and encouragement to adapt themselves to the market. They need jobs, and society pays a price for the frustration they experience when reasonable efforts to prepare for and find work prove futile. Turned inward, their frustration is self-destructive. Turned outward, it is likely to become antisocial. In either case, the social costs are considerable.

An EAP jobs program would provide both an appropriate and a constructive response to problems of this kind. The social costs associated with forcing extended idleness on potentially productive workers would be avoided, and society could provide itself with useful public goods and services as a bonus. There is a danger, though, that an EAP jobs program could become a second-class employment ghetto in which large numbers of structurally unemployed workers would be permanently trapped.

Two strategies could be adopted to combat this danger. The first would be to attach a high priority on the placement of all structurally unemployed EAP participants in regular private or public sector jobs, knowing that newly redundant workers would take their place in the program. The conception underlying this approach would be to see the program as a kind of recycling station in the labor market for workers needing training or retraining. The second strategy would be intentionally to create enough relatively permanent EAP jobs to absorb the economy's structural job deficit, making those jobs as indistinguishable as possible from other forms of government employment.

The two strategies could and probably should be combined. The optimal mixture of the two would depend on how rapidly structural change was occurring in the economy and on how long a particular job deficit was expected to last. Extensive continuing structural change would support reliance on the first strategy. The existence of a long-term structural job deficit would support reliance on the second. Certainly over the past two decades, a more or less permanent job deficit has existed in the United States. Whatever the future may hold, a more adequate policy response to this problem is currently needed.

In this context it is also appropriate to note that the burden of structural unemployment falls especially heavily on the shoulders of disadvantaged ethnic, gender, and age groups in society. The benefits of an EAP jobs program would therefore tend to be distributed in proportion to the disadvantages that the regular labor market visits on different groups. The program would therefore provide a means of delivering substantial remedial assistance to disadvantaged groups, but it would do so in a manner that would probably be more readily accepted by the public than other forms of affirmative action.[9]

ANTIPOVERTY EFFECTS

There is broad agreement regarding the characteristics of a good antipoverty program.[10] First, eligibility standards should be equitable. People in like circumstances should be treated alike (horizontal equity), and the level of assistance provided should be proportional to relative need (vertical equity). Second, the program should be target-appropriate and efficient. It should be responsive to the differing needs of different categories of recipients, it should deliver assistance in forms appropriate to those differing needs, and it should do so at minimum cost. Third, the program should be "need adequate." Simply put, aid levels should be sufficient to allow the poor to live in dignity. Fourth, the program should not have undesirable side effects. In particular, it should not undermine either the work ethic or family unity.

Current antipoverty programs use a variety of income maintenance benefits to achieve these ends. The approach is largely unproblematic when applied to those whom public opinion does not expect to work for wages. When income maintenance benefits are used to relieve poverty among employable persons, however, conflicts arise between the policy goals enumerated above. Most significantly, the goal of encouraging the work ethic is seen as conflicting with other policy goals.

The policy choices that must be made among competing priorities in this context are never satisfying. Aid levels tend to be inadequate. Eligibility requirements tend to violate principles of both horizontal and vertical equity. Either target efficiency is sacrificed for administrative efficiency or vice versa, and the integrity of the family is frequently undermined. The predictable result is endemic frustration and dissatisfaction with the programs among beneficiaries, administrators, and the public alike. Then, because they fall so far short of their goals, the programs become easy targets for those who advocate reductions in public assistance for the poor.[11]

Viewed as an antipoverty program for employable persons and their dependents, an EAP jobs program would not suffer from these weaknesses. Such a program could be need-adequate without undermining the work ethic. Eligibility requirements would be clear, equitable, target-efficient, and self-enforcing, since the entitlement would be based on the same willingness to work that conditions the receipt of income in the private labor market. All who need help could get it, but nothing would be given away. Family stability would not be undermined. To the contrary, families would be afforded the dignity of being able to support themselves. Also, by shielding families from the corrosive effects of poverty and unemployment, one of the major causes of familial collapse (and an inhibition to family formation) would be eliminated.

An EAP jobs program would attack the causes of poverty among employable persons rather than merely alleviating its effects. It would allow the able-bodied poor to work their way out of poverty, rather than eroding their self-reliance and their self-respect. It would provide them with what they need most and want most to maintain normal lives—work at living wages—rather than a mere offer to pick up the pieces of their broken lives.

There is good reason to believe that the nonemployable poor would also benefit from the establishment of an EAP jobs program. Current antipoverty programs obscure the distinction between those who are poor because they lack work and those who are poor because they cannot work. This tends to neutralize the public's greater natural sympathy for the latter group. Reaction to Reagan administration efforts to cut benefit programs for the elderly and the disabled in the early 1980s demonstrate that the public does support the provision of such aid. It is the provision of gratuitous income maintenance benefits to able-bodied persons of working age that is resented. If gratuitous aid were provided only to the elderly and the disabled (and to children lacking the support of both of their parents), then it is not unreasonable to expect that such aid would become more generous.

In addition, an EAP jobs program would provide more immediate benefits to the elderly and the disabled. Individuals from both these groups could choose to work in the program, at jobs suited to their capabilities, instead of receiving gratuitous public assistance. Many of them would strongly prefer to do so. An EAP jobs program could make a substantial contribution to the quality of their lives by affording them employment opportunities tailored to their special circumstances.

An EAP jobs program would also benefit both the working and the nonworking poor through the services it provided. It must not be forgotten that those employed in an EAP jobs program would not just be taking home paychecks. They would be providing the community with services, and these could include the full range of community services that policy analysts say are needed by the poor but that currently seem to be beyond our fiscal reach.

Thus, there is good reason to believe that combining employment assurance (for those who lack work) with traditional income maintenance benefits (for those whom society does not expect to work) would constitute a more effective antipoverty policy than current programs. The real puzzle is why developed market economies, despite their ideological commitment to the work ethic, seem more ready to use state finances to support the unemployed in forced idleness than to give them work. Cash and in-kind transfer payments are ubiquitous in capitalist welfare states. Government-financed employment programs are relatively rare.[12] Thus far, no persuasive justification for this seemingly irrational policy preference has become apparent.

CHAPTER 4

Economic Side Effects of an EAP Jobs Program

IN THE PREVIOUS chapter's discussion of the effectiveness of an EAP jobs program in combating unemployment and poverty, I did not take into consideration the possible economic side effects of the program. These could include general changes in wage and employment levels, both micro and macroeconomic efficiency effects, and the possibility of increased inflation. I shall consider each of these in turn.

WAGE AND EMPLOYMENT EFFECTS

If individuals could freely choose between EAP-funded jobs and those available in the regular labor market, one obvious result would be effectively to extend the protection of the federal minimum wage statute to workers who are either not covered by the statute or who are paid less than it requires in defiance of the law. About 10 percent of all nonsupervisory employees in the United States are presently not covered by the federal minimum wage statute. These workers include persons engaged in outside sales work, employees in some low-volume retail trade and service firms, and employees in seasonal amusement establishments. Most of them earn wages at least equal to the statutory minimum, despite their not being covered by the act, but a significant number do not. It has also been estimated that between 30 and 50 percent of workers who would have been paid less than the minimum wage in the absence of the federal statute are still paid less in violation of the law. Altogether, 1.6 million wage workers are known to be paid less than the current $3.35 federal minimum wage.[1]

An EAP jobs program would deliver substantial benefits to these workers. It would make the minimum wage statute largely self-enforcing and effectively extend its coverage to all workers by providing a wage floor that private employers would have to match to retain their laborforce. In addition, unlike a statutory extension of the act's coverage or a program of more vigorous regulatory enforcement of its standards, an EAP jobs program would ensure the continued availability of jobs for those low-wage workers who currently earn less than the minimum wage.

On the other hand, broadening the effective coverage of the minimum wage statute could reduce employment in the regular labor market, thereby increasing the cost of an EAP jobs program. Neoclassical theory predicts that by forcing wage rates above the equilibrium level, minimum wage statutes will cause increased unemployment among low-wage workers.[2] Econometric studies generally verify this result, though the observed effect is small. Typically, such studies find that a 10 percent increase in the statutory minimum wage results in a 1 to 3 percent decline in teenage employment but has little or no effect on adult employment. Those studies that distinguish between the effect of changes in the minimum wage rate and changes in the statute's coverage have found that the employment effects of the latter are even weaker.[3]

It cannot be concluded from this, however, that the general level of employment tends to be reduced by either an increase in the minimum wage or an extension of its coverage. This is because an increase in minimum wage rates may cause an increase in aggregate expenditures, and hence in total employment, even if low-wage employment declines.

First, neoclassical analysis predicts that an increase in minimum wages may increase total earnings for low-wage workers, even though employment levels for such workers decline. If the elasticity of demand for labor is less than one in a particular industry, then the additional earnings of workers whose wages are increased to comply with the statute will exceed the lost earnings of workers who lose their jobs.[4] If this happens, and the econometric studies cited above generally find this to be the case, then some redistribution of income in favor of low-wage workers is implied, even if no substitute income is provided for those who lose their jobs. Given the very high marginal propensity to consume of low-income earners, the result of this redistribution is likely to be an increase in aggregate consumption expenditures and a corresponding tendency for aggregate employment to grow.

Second, neoclassical analysis also predicts that an increase in the statutory minimum wage may cause an increase in the demand for higher-wage labor.[5] This is because an increase in the cost of low-wage labor may result in a cost advantage for technologies using more highly skilled labor. As firms substitute new production techniques for old ones, their demand for higher-wage labor may increase. New capital investment will also be required, providing a stimulus for increased employment beyond the immediately affected industry.

Thus, the net effect of an increase in minimum wages on aggregate employment may be positive, even if low-wage jobs are lost. Indeed, the overall stimulus provided to the economy by such an increase may cause a net employment gain even among low-wage workers. In any case, there is no reason to believe that an EAP jobs program would necessarily be rendered more costly because of its tendency to extend the reach of minimum wage legislation. In fact, the existence of such a program would reduce the likelihood of that possibility. Under present circumstances, low-wage workers who lose their jobs because of an increase in the minimum wage (or an extension of its coverage) are likely to remain unemployed and to experience a dramatic decline in income. An EAP jobs program would ensure their continued employment, thus increasing the net gain in earnings received by low-wage workers. The general economic stimulus provided by increased consumption expenditures by low-wage workers would therefore be increased.

An EAP jobs program would probably also exert some upward pressure on the general level of wages, since the establishment of effective full employment would strengthen the general bargaining power of both unionized and nonunionized workers. The general inflationary effect of an increase in the level of wages will be considered later in this chapter. The question that is of concern at this point is the likely employment effect of such a general increase in wage levels.

The employment effect of a general increase in wages would be similar to that of an increase in statutory minimum wage rates. On the one hand, increasing the cost of labor relative to other factors of production would tend to reduce the demand for labor in the regular labor market. On the other hand, the economic stimulus provided by increased consumption (due to increased wage payments) and increased investment (due to the substitution of capital for labor in the process of production) would tend to increase the demand for labor. Which tendency would predominate cannot be determined *a priori*, but the existence of an EAP jobs program would increase the likelihood that the net employment effect of a rising wage level would be positive. This is because such a program would ensure the continued employment of workers who lost their jobs as a result of the wage increase, thereby augmenting the increased earnings (and consequent consumption expenditures) of workers whose jobs were not eliminated.

An EAP jobs program that guaranteed working parents an income at least equal to the poverty line would also cause demographic shifts in the low-wage sector of the labor market. Parents employed in jobs paying less than they could earn in the jobs program would presumably abandon those jobs in order to seek work in the program. This would create additional low-wage employment opportunities in the regular labor market for workers without dependent children, but low-wage working parents would be disproportionately represented in the EAP work force.

It is not clear how many workers there are in the low-wage sector of the economy trying to support families on minimum wage jobs. In 1986 the total number of workers with hourly wages at or below the federal minimum of $3.35 per hour included 283 thousand husbands, 1 million wives, 337 thousand women who maintain families without husbands present, and twenty-nine thousand men who maintain families without wives present. Thus, the employed laborforce included 1.7 million family heads or coheads earning the minimum wage or less. The number of persons earning $4.35 per hour or less included 5.6 million family heads or coheads (1.1 million husbands, 3.4 million wives, 1 million women who maintain families, and 129 thousand men who maintain families).[6]

Unfortunately, these figures do not indicate how many of these low-wage husbands and wives have dependent children, nor the average size of the low-wage families counted (whether headed by a married couple or a parent without a spouse present). It is therefore impossible to say how many of these workers would have been eligible for EAP jobs paying above market wages. These figures provide an outside boundary, however, for the number of persons presently employed in the regular labor market who might be drawn into an EAP jobs program by the prospect of earning above-market wages, thereby creating an equal number of private sector vacancies for workers without children who would otherwise have to rely on the jobs program.

As I noted in my discussion of this phenomenon in chapter 2, a restoration of the federal minimum wage to its historic level would probably reduce this tendency to negligible proportions, because a higher minimum wage would mean that only low-wage workers with exceptionally large families would be eligible for above-market wages in EAP-funded jobs. If, however, large demographic shifts did occur in the laborforce due to the availability of above-market EAP wages for low-income parents, then the implications for the program would be substantial.

First, women with children would be disproportionately represented among EAP job-holders. Instead of being just an employment program, it would become the institutional focal point of society's response to the so-called feminization of poverty. This could pose a problem for the program if it succeeded to the negative image of the AFDC program, but it could have the opposite effect if program participants were viewed by the public as working parents struggling to support their children. The concentration of family heads among program participants would also facilitate the delivery of special support services to their families. In other words, a demographic concentration of single mothers in the program could be beneficial, but it would also present public relations risks.

A second effect of the demographic shifts in the low-wage work force that the program might cause would be an opening up of employment opportunities for unemployed workers without children in the low-wage sector of the regular labor market. The major beneficiaries of this trend would be low-skilled youthful workers, the group in the economy that currently experiences the highest rates of unemployment of any age cohort. Employers would be forced to hire greater numbers of such persons because of the movement of low-wage parents into the EAP laborforce.

For those concerned that an EAP jobs program would become a permanent low-wage ghetto for disadvantaged youths, this tendency would be reassuring. It would tend to ensure that a broad range of employment opportunities would be available to such youths, beyond those available in the jobs program itself. Low-wage working parents would have the same choice, of course, but they would tend to be attracted to the jobs program because of the higher wages they could earn there.

EFFICIENCY EFFECTS

Before discussing the efficiency effects of an EAP jobs program, some clarification is needed regarding the meaning of the concept of economic efficiency itself. Because of the influence exerted by neoclassical economic theory on policy analysis in the United States, a tendency exists to assume that economic efficiency necessarily means the maximization of market output relative to market input, both measured in monetary terms. This definition of economic efficiency is derived from the profit-maximizing goal ascribed to individual firms in neoclassical theory. To regard the efficient realization of this goal as an analogue for all forms of economic efficiency, however, effectively ignores other economic goals that are worthy of pursuit and devalues a wide range of nonmonetary costs associated with market-oriented economic activity. The normative judgement implicit in this restricted vision of economic efficiency is rarely scrutinized.

Efficiency is an engineering concept that relates outputs to inputs in a quantitative relationship. In order to use the concept, a decision must be made regarding the specific outputs and inputs to be measured, like miles per gallon, miles per hour, or carbon dioxide emissions per gallon or mile. This involves a decision based on the nature of one's interest in the process, and, as the above examples suggest, may reveal differences in the value systems of different optimizers.

In defining the concept of economic efficiency, a similar choice must be made regarding the nature of the outputs and inputs that it is thought desirable for society to maximize and minimize. Economic efficiency does not necessarily mean the maximization of monetary output relative to monetary input. To assume that it does involves making a value judgment regarding the perceived purpose of economic activity. Analysts who attach greater importance to the distributional effects of an economic process than to its effect on GNP or market competitiveness are not thereby expressing a willingness to sacrifice "economic efficiency" for the sake of achieving certain equity goals. They are defining economic efficiency as the maximization of those equity goals relative to some set of inputs or opportunity costs that they think it is desirable to minimize.

Rational policy analysis needs to be self-conscious regarding its assumptions and it needs to be prepared to justify them. Uncritical acceptance of the neoclassical definition of economic efficiency violates this principle and hinders the development of fully reasoned policy recommendations by prejudging a vitally important and clearly debatable issue, namely, the question of what standards it is most appropriate to apply in judging an economy's performance.

Despite misgivings on this score, I am going to use the concept of economic efficiency in its conventional sense in the discussion that follows. This decision stems partly from limitations of space, which prevent a thorough critique and reformulation of the concept of economic efficiency, and partly from the fact that questions regarding the possible negative side effects of an EAP jobs program are rooted in a neoclassical vision of the economy, and I feel bound to address those concerns.

There are three efficiency effects that I shall discuss in this context. The first is the effect of an EAP jobs program on the microeconomic efficiency of labor. The second is its effect on the competitiveness of particular industries, both domestically and internationally. The third is its effect on the macroeconomic efficiency of the economy.

The Microeconomic Efficiency of Labor

What effect would an EAP jobs program have on the productivity of labor relative to its cost? In addressing that question I will assume that an EAP jobs program would exert upward pressure on wages, especially in low-wage industries, while simultaneously increasing labor's sense of security and independence. Put baldly, I will assume that workers would be less fearful of displeasing their employers.

It is possible that under such circumstances worker discipline and effort would diminish, thereby lessening the productivity of labor, but such a result is far from certain. Economic security improves worker morale and may lead to less interest in "feather bedding" on the part of labor. Both of these tendencies can increase the productivity of labor. Unions might take advantage of their increased bargaining strength to wrest productivity-lessening concessions from management, but with the achievement of full employment there would be less reason for unions to press for the maintenance of work rules designed mainly to save jobs rather than to achieve an intrinsically desirable pace of labor. Moreover, recent research calls into question the widely held assumption that strong unions reduce labor productivity in any case.[7]

The same disparity in possible outcomes also exists for individual workers. Employers would clearly have to rely more on the carrot and less on the stick in their relations with their employees, but it is difficult to say what effect this would have on productivity. In short, worker discipline and effort are complexly determined variables, and it is hard to predict what effect an EAP jobs program would have on them.

There is another efficiency effect of rising wages, however, which is more certain to occur. This is the encouragement that rising wages would provide for the introduction of labor-saving or labor-displacing technological and organizational innovations in the production process. These innovations will tend to increase the physical productivity of labor, whether or not the monetary costs of production decline below the levels experienced before the wage increase.[8] From the firm's point of view, innovations of this type may simply mitigate the decline in economic efficiency caused by the wage increase, but from society's point of view the result is a clear gain in the economy's overall efficiency, so long as displaced workers find alternative employment that is at least as productive as their old work. The reason the efficiency gain may not be realized at the firm level is because workers have captured it in their prior wage gain.

All of this is simply a roundabout way of saying that real investment increases the efficiency of an economy, and wage gains can induce real investment. The reason for this is twofold. First, rising wages may render technological innovations profitable that would not otherwise be so. Second, a rising wage level may result in an increase in aggregate consumption, which in turn induces increased real investment.[9]

Industrial Competitiveness

Regardless of the effect of an EAP jobs program on aggregate economic efficiency, individual industries could be harmed by a tendency for wages to rise. This would be especially true in the low-wage sector of the economy where the largest wage increases would be likely to occur. Indeed, there may be industries or individual firms whose survival depends on their access to low-wage labor. This could be the case because of foreign competition or because demand for the goods and services they sell is extremely price-elastic. In either case, if an EAP jobs program caused wages to rise significantly in the low-wage sector of the labor market and compensating technological innovations were unavailable, the industry or firm could experience substantial harm.

If foreign competition is the source of the problem, then the issue posed would be no different from the much-debated one of whether a protectionist trade policy should be adopted to save particular industries. Orthodox trade theory asserts that an across-the-board decline in domestic industries cannot follow from a free trade policy (unless the rest of the world is willing to subsidize a nation's consumption indefinitely through ever larger foreign exchange lending). Some industries will decline as foreign producers take over their markets, but export industries will just as surely expand to satisfy the growing demand created by larger dollar holdings by foreigners. In other words, structural change will occur in the economy.[10]

Arguments can be made that particular structural changes are undesirable, but for a diversified industrial economy, the issue usually boils down to one of competing private interests. How much harm will a free trade policy visit on losers in a structural reorganization of the economy? Will there be more gainers than losers? Can the latter be compensated? Will they be compensated?

The existence of an EAP jobs program could materially affect the resolution of these issues. By providing substitute employment for workers who lose their jobs as a result of trade-induced structural changes in the domestic economy, such a program would provide an automatic mechanism for compensating the largest group of potential "losers" in an open economy. It would also provide an ongoing institutional mechanism for assisting those workers to find different jobs, enter different professions, or move to different communities. Finally, it would provide long-term employment to fill any residual structural employment deficit.

This latter point is particularly important. Even if exports tend to grow apace with imports, it does not necessarily follow that employment growth in export industries will compensate for job losses in declining industries. That will depend on the relative labor intensity of the affected industries (as well as on differences in the multiplier effect of changes in income in each industry). A growth in petroleum product exports of $100 million need not create as many new jobs as would be lost from a decline in garment industry sales of equal magnitude.

The existence of a permanent institutional structure capable of delivering effective compensation to displaced workers could have a significant impact on public debate regarding trade policy, by reducing political support for protectionist measures among workers. This would provide small comfort, of course, to the owners of businesses harmed by foreign competition. Their opposition to free trade policies would continue, unless they too were compensated.

Even if a low-wage industry faced no international competition, it might still be squeezed by rising wages attributable to an EAP jobs program. The nature of the effect would depend on how industry sales were affected by two counteracting tendencies attributable to a wage increase. The first is an increase in consumer income. The second is an increase in the price of whatever goods or services the industry sells. Since price increases induced by rising wages would be greatest in those industries that employ the highest proportion of low-wage workers, whereas increased sales would be more evenly distributed throughout the economy, total revenues in low-wage industries would probably decline. If this happened, then total revenues in other industries would increase disproportionately, compared to the increase in their labor costs (since increased consumer income would have to be spent on something). A structural change would occur in the economy involving a reallocation of productive resources from lower-wage to higher-wage industries.

Would this be desirable or undesirable? Consider the population groups most likely to be harmed by rising prices and declining employment in low-wage industries. They include low-wage workers, consumers of low-wage goods and services, and employers of low-wage labor. Because workers laid off from declining industries would be able to take EAP-funded jobs, they would retain the benefit of the upward trend in wages. On the other hand, consumers of the products of low-wage labor would experience a slight decline in their real income. Finally, employers of low-wage labor would experience possibly substantial decreases in their sales or profits.

If, for example, the wages of migrant farmworkers increased, the price of agricultural products would go up slightly, and the real income of consumers of agricultural products would go down slightly. They would probably respond by buying fewer agricultural products. If they did, some farm workers would lose their jobs. Given the availability of EAP-funded jobs paying market wages, the laid-off farmworkers would be guaranteed continued employment at the higher wages that started the process. The increased expenditures of the farmworker population (attributable to their higher wages, whether or not they were all still working in their old jobs) would increase sales and employment in some other industries.

When the process was complete, the low-wage agricultural sector would be slightly smaller, some other sectors of the economy would be slightly larger, consumers who were not farmworkers would have experienced a slight decline in real income, with the benefits of the redistribution of income going to the farmworkers. Such a result seems supportable on equitable grounds. The only party that might experience significant economic harm would be employers of low-wage labor. If compensation is thought to be needed for such persons, it could be provided.

Macroeconomic Efficiency

Most discussions of economic efficiency focus on microeconomic performance. The unstated assumption is that because commodity x is more efficiently produced, the economy is more efficient. This is not necessarily true. The overall efficiency of the economy depends only partly on the average productivity of employed workers. It is also affected by the proportion of the laborforce that is employed. Put simply, a firm will become more efficient if, all other things remaining equal, it reduces the amount of labor it uses to produce a given output; but the efficiency of the laborforce taken as a whole will not increase in that instance unless redundant workers are provided alternative employment.

This is one of the reasons why centrally planned economies are often able to achieve high rates of economic growth despite the much-publicized inefficiencies of their individual enterprises. By keeping their entire laborforce productively employed, such economies offset losses attributable to firm-level inefficiencies. Clearly, their economies would be more efficient if they combined firm-level efficiency with full employment, but the same is true of capitalist economies.

An EAP jobs program provides an institutional means for achieving this goal. By substituting productive employment for transfer payments, an EAP jobs program would cause aggregate real income to increase. More goods and services would be produced, while the size of the laborforce (counting both employed and unemployed workers) remained constant. The efficiency of the laborforce taken as a whole would therefore increase. This would be true whether or not the productivity of EAP jobholders equaled that of persons employed in regular labor market jobs, since some production is greater than no production.

In national income accounts, GNP would increase to the extent that EAP jobs program expenditures replaced gratuitous income maintenance benefits. This would show up in the accounts as an increase in government purchases of goods and services, accompanied by a corresponding decrease in government transfer payments. The changes would be real, however, not nominal. More goods and services would be produced in the economy. Society's real income would increase.

INFLATIONARY EFFECTS

It is widely believed that the achievement of genuine full employment would be inflationary. This is why so many economists have tried to redefine the concept of full employment to mean the level of employment necessary to keep inflation in check. It is therefore to be expected that most people would regard it as a foregone conclusion that an EAP jobs program would be inflationary.

In fact, such a result is not as certain as it seems. There is no reason to doubt that under the existing policy regime substantial inflationary pressures would be unleashed by the achievement of full employment. What is less clear is whether the cause of that inflationary tendency is properly attributable to full employment itself or to the high level of expenditures necessary to achieve it spontaneously. Stated differently, there would be much less reason to fear the inflationary effects of full employment if it were not necessary to expand aggregate expenditures to achieve it.

If my earlier analysis of the financing of an EAP jobs program is correct, then the fiscal stimulus provided by the program would be negligible. Over the course of the business cycle, government spending for EAP jobs would be almost entirely offset by a combination of reductions in spending for other programs and of increased tax revenues from the earnings of program participants. If the program's residual funding deficit were financed by increased taxes or by user fees for the services it provided, then it should have no long-term fiscal impact at all. Moreover, the countercyclical timing of program expenditures might even cause it to have an antiinflationary effect. Program expenditures would exceed tax revenues only in periods of depressed demand, while at the peak of the business cycle program expenditures would be less than the tax receipts dedicated to its support.

Thus, for the achievement of full employment through the mechanism of an EAP jobs program to be inflationary, it would have to be because of the program's effect on wage levels. That is, upward pressure on wage levels attributable to the program would have to lead to a general rise in prices. It is not clear, though, how robust a wage-price spiral could be in the absence of any net fiscal or monetary stimulus. The inflation associated with wage-price spirals may appear to be self-generating, but without some fiscal or monetary accommodation it could not be sustained for very long.

Any wage-price spiral generated by an EAP jobs program would be driven solely by the program's effect on the relative bargaining power of employers and workers, and not conjointly by expansive fiscal or monetary policies. In other words, an EAP-induced wage-price spiral would amount to nothing more than a fight over income shares set off by the program's redistributive tendencies. Once market adjustments to the new distribution of income had worked their way through the economy, there would be no further inflationary pressure unless further redistributions of income in favor of low-wage labor occurred, or unless an effort were made to defeat the real effects of the redistribution by adopting inflationary fiscal or monetary policies.

To understand this better, it is worth considering the actual mechanism whereby an EAP jobs program might initiate a wage-price spiral. As noted earlier, such a program would tend to increase the real income of low-wage earners while reducing the net income of low-wage employers. To the degree that the latter were able to pass along their increased labor costs in the form of higher prices, they would recoup part of their loss by shifting it to the consuming public generally. A similar scenario would unfold if an EAP jobs program led to rising wages in other than the low-wage sector of the economy. Some inflation would occur, but there is no reason that it should continue once the redistributive effects of an EAP jobs program had run their course. For a wage-price spiral to continue indefinitely would mean that the fight for income shares among workers, employers, and consumers had not died down.

This does not mean that the short-term inflationary pressures unleashed by the establishment of an EAP jobs program would necessarily be minor. As the history of oil price increases in the 1970s illustrates, struggles over income shares fought out through market mechanisms can have a major impact on the economy. On the other hand, the existence of an EAP jobs program would make it easier to use other policy weapons to fight any inflation the economy did experience. This is because the program would tend to unburden fiscal and monetary policy from the need to focus simultaneous attention on the problems of unemployment and inflation.

It has become commonplace for economists to observe that they know how to reduce either the rate of inflation or the rate of unemployment, but they have trouble doing both at the same time. With adequate support for the unemployed being provided by an EAP jobs program, they wouldn't have to try to do both at the same time. The traditional tools of macroeconomic policy could be deployed more singlemindedly to combat inflation, whatever its cause, while the costs of the antiinflation effort—in the form of lost jobs—would be shared by the entire population through increased EAP expenditures, rather than being laid disproportionately on the shoulders of the unemployed.

Also, since any prolonged EAP-induced inflation would reflect an ongoing battle over income shares, a strong case can be made for supplementing antiinflationary macroeconomic policy, when necessary, with some form of active incomes policy. After all, antipoverty measures are themselves a form of incomes policy, and if we really are serious about altering the market-induced distribution of income to ensure that everyone has the right to a modest subsistence, then we have already decided to interfere in market processes.

Incomes policies attempt to influence wages and prices directly by bringing moral, political, or legal pressures to bear on economic behavior, or by altering the institutional framework in which market mechanisms work. Antiinflationary interventions have traditionally taken a variety of forms, ranging from the publication of guidelines to the establishment of legal controls. The government can also use its taxing power to reward or deter certain kinds of wage- and price-setting behavior, or it can intervene as a mediator or as a direct participant in wage and price bargaining in the private sector.[11]

For such policies to be successfully deployed to combat inflation, a high degree of popular support is needed. Where the goals that necessitate the policies are widely supported, as was the case with wage and price controls during the Second World War, they can work. When no such support exists, as was the case with wage and price controls in the early 1970s, incomes policies are not likely to survive public resentment. Thus, whether an incomes policy could be used successfully as a supplement to macroeconomic policy in fighting the inflationary tendencies of an EAP jobs program would depend primarily on political rather than technical considerations.

Finally, in weighing the importance of the inflationary effect of an EAP jobs program, it is important to cast an equally appraising eye on existing policies. By placing primary reliance on fiscal and monetary policy to fight both inflation and unemployment, we are currently trapped between the proverbial rock and a hard place. We can't achieve both goals at once. Since the immediately perceived effects of inflation are felt by a larger proportion of the population than are those associated with unemployment, and because they are felt by groups with more political influence than that exercised by the unemployed, a strong tendency exists to accept high rates of unemployment as the price of keeping inflation in check.

This strategy is undoubtedly effective, but it is hard to justify on equitable grounds, and if my analysis is correct, it is equally hard to justify on grounds of the public's actual self-interest. It amounts to the imposition of an extremely harsh economic sanction on a minority of the population for the sake of preserving the perceived economic welfare of the majority. But given the cost to society of unemployment itself, the bargain is a very expensive one, even for the majority.

If there were no alternative means of overcoming inflationary tendencies in a market economy, such a policy regime might be defensible, but if alternative means are available to fight inflation without sacrificing the goal of full employment, then it becomes far more difficult to justify our willingness to sacrifice the unemployed and to live with the costs of unemployment in order to achieve price stability.

In other words, existing policies no less than the alternatives I have suggested involve difficult choices regarding antiinflation policy. An EAP jobs program would pose problems in this area, but it is by no means certain that they would be more serious than those we currently face as a result of our stop-and-go efforts to fight both inflation and unemployment with macroeconomic weapons that clearly have trouble doing both jobs at once. Rather than being its Achilles' heel, the effect of an EAP jobs program on our ability to control inflation may be an advantage of the policy.

CHAPTER 5

Administrative Problems and Opportunities

THE ESTABLISHMENT of an EAP jobs program would pose a number of difficult administrative problems. Some of these would flow from the sheer size of the program. In 1985, for example, I have estimated that the program's budget would have been five times as great as that of the U.S. Postal Service, and it would have employed fourteen times as many people.[1] Any government program of that size would be difficult to administer.

In considering the administrative problems associated with the operation of an EAP jobs program, however, it must be kept in mind that such a program would also reduce some existing administrative problems. In the first instance, it would reduce the administrative burden of running those social welfare programs that a jobs program would either partially or wholly replace. Second, and perhaps more important, it would reduce the general administrative burden of coping with a host of seemingly intractable economic, social, medical, and psychological problems that are associated with unemployment and poverty. The question that needs to be asked is not whether it would be difficult to run an EAP jobs program, but whether it would be more difficult to run such a program than to achieve similarly positive results utilizing the existing institutions of the modern welfare state.

With that caveat in mind, it is time to consider the particular administrative problems that an EAP jobs program would have to address. These include the so-called fiscal substitution problem that figured prominently in criticism of public employment programs in the late 1970s, the problem of defining and regulating the relationship between EAP jobs and regular employment in the public sector, the problem of defining and applying eligibility criteria for continued receipt of gratuitous income maintenance benefits, the problem of finding useful work for EAP jobholders to do, and the problem of maintaining worker discipline in a program that guarantees jobs for all applicants. I shall consider each of these problems in turn.

THE FISCAL SUBSTITUTION PROBLEM

One of the criticisms most frequently directed at the public employment programs established during the 1970s under the authority of the Comprehensive Employment and Training Act (CETA) was that their job-creating effect was greatly reduced or even nullified by the tendency of municipal governments to use the program to provide services that would have been provided anyway at local taxpayer expense. The actual extent of this fiscal substitution effect has been much debated. Contentions that the effect was large are supported by econometric studies conducted early in the program's history,[2] but later case study and survey research have suggested that the earlier econometric studies overstated the actual extent of the problem.[3] It was the early perceptions of the fiscal substitution problem, though, which were most influential in determining the program's fate. They were partly responsible for a major statutory modification of the program in 1978, and they were also cited in justification of the program's termination in the early 1980s.[4]

Whatever fiscal substitution effect CETA programs did have, the problem could be worse for an EAP jobs program. One reason for this is because an EAP jobs program would be several times as large as CETA.[5] More importantly, several of the administrative features included in CETA after 1978 to discourage fiscal substitution would be harder to incorporate into an EAP jobs program. For example, an EAP jobs program could not limit eligibility to the hard-core structurally unemployed without defeating its countercyclical purpose. Also, placing a time limit on individual participation would violate the guaranteed employment feature of the program. Limiting work activities to self-terminating projects would also not be possible for crucial EAP activities (such as the provision of child care) and would squander opportunities to use the program to improve public services. Finally, relying on the private nonprofit sector to provide program jobs would be unrealistic for such a large program, and it would make program auditing more difficult. Given these limitations, what steps could or should be taken to minimize the fiscal substitution effects of an EAP jobs program?

In answering that question, two points must be kept in mind. The first is that fiscal substitution is not undesirable under all circumstances. The phenomenon actually embodies two effects. One is a reduction in the net employment effect of federally financed job-creation programs. The other is a shift in the burden of financing state and local government services. Each of these effects warrants analysis. Even if a particular jobs program were found to have no net employment effect, it still might have a positive equity effect by providing for a more equal sharing of tax burdens among wealthy and poor communities, relative to the quantity and quality of public services they each provide. If this were the case, the fiscal substitution phenomenon might be deemed desirable, despite its ineffectiveness in achieving its stated goal of reducing unemployment rates.

The second point that must be kept in mind in assessing the fiscal substitution problem is that the tendency is not inherent in all public employment programs. It is a problem that is largely attributable to the practice of having the federal government pay for employment programs, while vesting administrative control over them in state or local governments. When one level of government foots the bill, while another controls the expenditure of the funds, fiscal substitution is likely to be a problem. Under these circumstances, state and local officials are faced with the very tempting option of using the program as a form of general revenue-sharing. By assigning program enrollees duties that would otherwise have to be performed at local expense, local officials can shift the burden of paying for local government services to the federal government.

Thus, in assessing the fiscal substitution effects of an EAP jobs program, it is necessary to consider both the issue of tax equity and the question of how control over the program should be distributed among different levels of government.

Fiscal Substitution and Tax Equity

If properly controlled, the fiscal substitution effect of an EAP jobs program could enhance tax equity. Indeed, inherent differences in the likely fiscal substitution behavior of rich and poor communities would naturally tend to work in this direction. This is because the fiscal substitution opportunities presented by an EAP jobs program would be roughly proportional to the unemployment rate in a community. Since wealthy communities tend to have lower unemployment rates than poor ones, their capacity to substitute EAP job-holders for regular government employees would also be less than that of poor communities. Thus, the poorer the community, the greater would be the fiscal substitution opportunities presented by an EAP jobs program.

Therefore, within bounds, the relatively greater tendency of poor communities to practice fiscal substitution might be welcomed as beneficial. Wealthy communities tend to have low rates of taxation (measured against income or wealth) relative to the quantity and the quality of the government services they provide. When such communities practice fiscal substitution, it almost surely results in a regressive shifting of tax burdens. When poor communities pursue a similar policy, however, the result is likely to be a shift in tax burdens that increases tax equity.

Since the primary purpose of a public employment program is to create jobs, any contribution that the program might make to tax equity is not likely to be seen as important unless the employment-generating effects of the program can also be preserved. This was certainly the case with reference to CETA. If the employment-generating effects of a public employment program could be guaranteed, though, then the tax-shifting effects of the fiscal substitution phenomenon might be deemed acceptable or even desirable.

Consider, for example, the implications of totally unleashed fiscal substitution under an EAP jobs program. Local governments would first provide what services they could using the labor of EAP participants. Services that could not be provided in this fashion would have to be funded by local taxes. Local taxation would therefore come to function, in effect, as a supplement to federal funding of local government services, with the federal assistance being distributed in direct proportion to a community's unemployment rate (and hence to its probable need). Federal tax revenues would have to be increased, of course, but only to the degree that local taxes were reduced, and this too would work to the advantage of poorer communities because of the greater progressivity of federal income taxes as compared to most sources of local revenue. In other words, the net effect of uncontrolled fiscal substitution under these circumstances would be a rationalization of the nation's tax system in a progressive direction.

With this in mind, the appropriate policy goal for an EAP jobs program might not be to prevent fiscal substitution, but merely to limit it. A general prohibition of fiscal substitution that was loosely enforced might be sufficient. To be truly effective, a policy of concerted fiscal substitution would have to involve the shifting of currently employed municipal workers to the EAP payroll. Any large-scale efforts to do that would be fairly easy to detect, and more limited or subtle forms of fiscal substitution would probably shift tax burdens in a desirable direction for the reasons I have just elaborated.

If a more concerted effort to limit fiscal substitution was thought to be necessary for political reasons, then further limitations on local discretion would have to be enforced. In analyzing how this could best be done, however, it is important to consider the second feature of the fiscal substitution problem noted above.

Fiscal Substitution and Federalism

If state and local governments did not have the authority to determine local levels of taxation, the fiscal substitution problem would not exist. Nor would it exist if state and local governments did not control the level of services they provide. Finally, the scope of the problem depends on the degree of control exercised by state and local governments over the work assignments of enrollees in public employment programs. In short, the opportunity for fiscal substitution is created by the combination of federal financing with state or local government control of (1) state or local levels of taxation, (2) the nature and level of state or local government services provided, or (3) the work assignments given to employment program enrollees. Discouraging fiscal substitution therefore requires some limitation on local government discretion in one or more of these areas.

One strategy for doing this would be to focus regulatory attention on local government employment levels and patterns. A prohibition on the substitution of EAP job-holders for regular government employees would fall under this heading. Enforcement of such a prohibition would require some form of monitoring of local government employment practices, a mechanism that was mandated under CETA.

There are serious problems, however, with this strategy of discouraging fiscal substitution. The services that local governments need to provide necessarily change over time. Population growth or shrinkage, changes in the age distribution of the population, changes in the nature of a community's economy, and other analogous developments can all affect the absolute level and mix of services that local governments must offer. To regard local government employment patterns at the time an EAP jobs program was established as a baseline for measuring ongoing obligations is simply unrealistic. Other standards would have to be introduced over time, and that raises the question of what those standards should be.

A second strategy for discouraging fiscal substitution would be to use tax rates to measure the ongoing fiscal responsibilities of local governments. This would provide a standard less subject to change over time than local government employment patterns, and it would also be better suited to the task of distinguishing between desirable and undesirable fiscal substitution.

In general, the lower the average income of a community's population, the higher its effective tax rates must be to generate a given level of per capita tax revenue. The result is that poorer communities find it more difficult to provide a given level of government services than do richer communities. A town whose residents enjoy an average family income of $100,000 a year can provide an average of $5,000 worth of government services to each resident family by taxing income at an effective 5 percent rate. A town whose residents enjoy an average family income of only $20,000 a year would have to impose taxes five times as great to afford the same level of services.

Thus, as a means of equalizing tax burdens among communities relative to the quantity and quality of government services they provide, poor communities with high effective tax rates could be permitted some latitude for fiscal substitution, while wealthier communities could be denied that opportunity.

A third means of controlling the problem of fiscal substitution would be to adopt the prevailing New Deal practice of having the federal government itself administer the public employment programs it finances. Under such an arrangement, state and local governments could still assume primary responsibility for project selection, but their choice of projects would be more easily monitored to forestall fiscal substitution.[6]

In the WPA, for example, the vast majority of all projects were sponsored by local governments. The sponsors not only applied for certain projects to be funded; they assumed responsibility for planning the work that was to be undertaken. They had to prepare all blueprints, to detail the tasks to be performed by WPA workers, and to specify the size and type of workforce needed. They then helped to direct the projects, paying an average of 20 percent of their total cost (typically by providing materials).[7]

WPA workers were federal employees, though, under the control of supervisors who were also employed by the WPA. This made it difficult for local officials to divert program staff to perform unapproved local services, while it still gave local governments substantial control over project selection in their communities.

With this administrative structure, fiscal substitution tendencies were relatively easy to control. All that was required were administrative guidelines specifying the kinds of activities that the employment program could not undertake (because it was presumed that they were the responsibility of state or local governments). Waivers of these restrictions were granted, however, when a local government's financial condition was so bad that it was deemed unable to assume its traditional responsibilities.[8]

There are also disadvantages to structuring an employment program in this way. It would, for example, prevent the integration of EAP job-holders into the regular local government workforce, thereby preventing the program from being used to improve and expand the delivery of traditional local government services. Also, it is an administrative structure best suited for carrying out discrete projects.

In summary, then, a variety of methods exist for limiting the fiscal substitution tendencies intrinsic to federally financed public employment programs. The administrative challenge would be to devise means of doing so that were both politically palatable and that placed as few constraints as possible on the use of the program to serve public needs. There are undoubtedly trade-offs to be faced between these two goals, and given the layered sharing of fiscal authority that exists among levels of government in the United States, no ideal solution to the problem can be claimed to exist. Still, there is no warrant for concluding that the problem is uncontrollable.

Public Sector Labor Relations

An issue closely related to the fiscal substitution problem is how regular government employees would respond to an EAP jobs program. If they saw the program as a threat to their jobs, their professional status, their wage levels, or to protections afforded under either civil service regulations or collective bargaining agreements, then they would probably oppose it.[9] Moreover, it is not unreasonable to fear such consequences. An EAP jobs program could be used by government agencies to undercut the position of their regular employees. Fiscal substitution by local governments is simply one example of such undercutting actions.

On the other hand, the more similar EAP employment was to regular public sector employment, the less cause existing government employees would have to fear the program. From the perspective of such employees, the ideal EAP jobs program would be one that simply provided funding for additional regular public sector hiring. If, under EAP auspices, government employment were simply expanded to provide jobs for unemployed workers, without altering the terms or conditions of that employment, then existing government employees would have no reason to fear the program. Indeed, they would probably welcome it, since workloads could be eased and new opportunities would be created for experienced workers to move into supervisory positions.[10] Even fiscal substitution would hold little sting for local government employees if all it meant was that the source of funding for their jobs shifted to Washington.

To a certain extent, an EAP jobs program paying market wages could operate in this way. Additional funding could be provided to existing government agencies, permitting them to expand their regular hiring. Normal hiring procedures would not have to be altered, because it would not matter whether the individuals hired were previously unemployed or not. Any jobs vacated by persons accepting a newly funded public sector position would thereby become available to other job-seekers. It would be important, though, to limit the public sector positions funded in this fashion to job categories for which significant numbers of unemployed persons were known to be qualified. Otherwise, the policy would merely contribute to labor shortages in certain sectors of the labor market.

In practice this would mean that existing agencies could expand their hiring of relatively unskilled labor to almost any level desired, but hiring in more specialized job categories would have to be accompanied by a commitment to train less-skilled workers to fill the positions.

The provision of entirely new government services (like child care) could also be funded in this fashion, so long as the personnel needs of the agencies providing the new services matched available supplies of unemployed labor. In other words, an EAP jobs program would not have to administer all of the new public services it would make possible, nor would all EAP-funded hiring have to involve special job application and assignment procedures. The program could instead provide the funding (either partial or total) necessary to establish new activities within other government agencies whose hiring practices would conform to normal public sector practice.

There are, however, two major considerations that would limit the use of this administrative strategy. The first is that it would aggravate the program's fiscal substitution problem. The more complete the integration of EAP and regularly funded positions within government agencies, the more difficult it would be to monitor and control fiscal substitution tendencies. Hence, this strategy would be practical only if it were limited to federal agencies, or if it were accompanied by very strong controls preventing undesirable fiscal substitution by state and local governments.

The second consideration is that additional public sector hiring of this type would not provide "employment assurance" for all individuals. Short-term work projects would still have to be established to meet the needs of seasonally and cyclically unemployed workers. Special employment programs would also be needed on a permanent basis for certain categories of workers (like sheltered workshops for disabled workers). Free-standing employment programs might also be deemed desirable (or necessary) to provide enough jobs for certain demographic groups, such as single youths, or for especially large geographic concentrations of structurally unemployed workers. Finally, if hiring procedures for positions that were funded by the jobs program while being administered by other government agencies conformed to normal public sector practices, then the jobs program itself would have to serve as employer of last resort for persons otherwise unable to find work or at least unable to find it at the minimum need-based wage rates we are assuming the program would pay to low-wage working parents.

It would also be possible, of course, to employ all EAP job-holders in work projects that were segregated from other government activities, thereby creating a strict distinction between regular public sector jobs and EAP-funded positions. If administrative controls were established that ensured that these projects did not displace regularly funded government activities, then opposition to the program by regular government employees would probably be minimal. This administrative structure was adopted by major New Deal employment programs such as the Civilian Conservation Corps (CCC), the Civil Works Administration (CWA), and the Works Progress Administration (WPA).[11]

ELIGIBILITY CRITERIA

Throughout this analysis it has been assumed that EAP jobs would be freely available to all who wanted them. Given that assumption, the only issue that needs to be addressed concerning eligibility criteria is how the line would be drawn between persons who are deemed eligible to receive traditional income maintenance benefits and those who are not.

The assumption adopted in my analysis of the fiscal feasibility of providing employment assurance was that eligibility for existing income maintenance benefits would be limited to the elderly, the disabled, and to children lacking the support of both their parents (due to the parents' death, disability, or absence from home). Defining disability is the only real problem in this model. It would not be a new problem, though, since it already exists in the administration of the Social Security Disability Insurance and Supplemental Security Income programs.

The Disability Insurance program (DI) provides income maintenance benefits to disabled workers who have achieved "fully insured" status within the Social Security system. The benefits provided are comparable to those paid under the Old Age and Survivors Insurance program (OASI), and neither a person's eligibility to receive benefits nor the level of benefits paid is subject to a means test. The Supplemental Security Income program (SSI) provides means-tested benefits for aged, blind, or disabled persons who are also poor.[12]

The definition of disability is the same for both DI and SSI. To be eligible for benefits a person must be unable to engage in any substantial gainful activity by reason of a medically determined physical or mental impairment that has lasted or is expected to last for at least twelve continuous months or is expected to end in the person's death. Administrative determinations of disability status result in a simple yes or no answer. No benefits are provided to partially disabled workers, and persons who do receive benefits are required to accept vocational rehabilitation services. Benefit payments are terminated if a recipient recovers the capacity to engage in substantial gainful activity, even if the recovery is partial and does not permit a resumption of the recipient's former occupation. To reduce work disincentives, though, benefits are only gradually withdrawn when a recipient reenters the workforce.[13]

In practice, it is exceedingly difficult to draw the line between those who reasonably can be expected to work and those who can't. Applicants have a strong incentive to be or seem to be as unwell as possible. On the other hand, program administrators are under strong political pressures to ensure that "undeserving" applicants do not receive benefits. They must therefore adopt a skeptical stance with respect to an applicant's claim. Under these circumstances, the eligibility determination process inevitably assumes an adversarial character that does little to advance the goal of encouraging persons with physical or mental disabilities to maximize their capabilities.[14]

There is no reason to believe that the administrative problems associated with the determination of disability status under these programs would become any more difficult following the establishment of an EAP jobs program. Indeed, the establishment of vocational rehabilitation and sheltered workshop programs under the EAP umbrella would create an opportunity to redesign these programs so as to better serve the needs of disabled workers, while simultaneously eliminating most of the problems currently associated with disability determination proceedings.

Specifically, a nonadversarial model for the delivery of public assistance to the disabled could be devised. Instead of making direct application for income transfer benefits, disabled individuals could be invited to apply to a special screening facility that would work with the applicant, in consultation with the applicant's doctor where that was appropriate, to develop a vocational rehabilitation or work program suited to the applicant's capacities and needs. It would no longer be necessary to make a simple yes or no determination regarding a person's capacity to engage in substantial gainful employment. Rather, an individualized vocational strategy could be devised for each applicant that was designed to maximize the person's well-being and self-esteem.

Critically ill or totally incapacitated applicants could be provided the equivalent of an EAP wage as a straight transfer payment. Severely disabled but not totally incapacitated applicants could be provided occupational therapy prescribed by their doctor as an adjunct to their medical or psychiatric treatment. Individuals with less severe disabilities could be offered enrollment in a full-time program of vocational training or a job in a sheltered workshop.

For some the goal of such a program would be to achieve full entry or reentry into the world of normal work. For others the goal would simply be to maximize the person's independence and self-esteem. All could receive regular EAP wages, conditioned only on their continued participation in the program, thereby assuring even the disabled the opportunity to "earn" enough to be self-supporting.

PROJECT SELECTION

An average of about sixteen million people were employed by all levels of government during the ten-year period that is the focus of my fiscal analysis.[15] During that same period I have estimated that an EAP jobs program would have needed to provide an average of about seven million full-time and about three million part-time jobs per year (table 2.4). Could productive work have been found for that many additional workers?

In theory, there should be no problem. Neoclassical economists maintain that our wants are limited only by resource scarcity. Given the availability of a prepaid multimillion-member laborforce, there should be no lack of wants demanding satisfaction, especially if there is any truth at all to the contention that market societies tend to underproduce public goods.[16] Be that as it may, the political and administrative task of putting that many people to work would be a formidable one.

To put the undertaking in perspective, however, it is useful to recall the accomplishments of the Roosevelt administration in establishing employment programs for unemployed workers in the 1930s. The Works Progress Administration (WPA) is the best known of those programs. Established in the summer of 1935, the WPA provided jobs for 3.3 million persons at its peak and was not finally terminated until 1943.[17] The New Deal's greatest administrative achievement in this area, though, was probably the successful establishment of the Civil Works Administration (CWA), a short-lived but substantially more ambitious predecessor of the WPA, which provided jobs for 4.3 million persons during the winter of 1933–34.[18]

The decision to establish the CWA on a temporary basis was made, with little advance planning, on 2 November 1933.[19] The task set for its administrators was a gargantuan one—to mobilize and usefully employ a workforce seven times as large as that of the entire federal government,[20] and to do it in a matter of weeks in the dead of a winter that proved to be one of the coldest on record.

Just arranging for paychecks to be printed and distributed required a major cooperative effort on the part of a number of government agencies. At the time the CWA was established, the federal government was writing about thirty-three million paychecks a year. During the next four-and-a-half months, an extra sixty million were issued. To ensure that the first batch of one million would be available on time, the president ordered several federal agencies to suspend normal operations in order to get the CWA work done. The Government Printing Office undertook its largest single order ever in delivering enough check-writing paper. The Bureau of Printing and Engraving scheduled triple shifts to print the checks, which were then transported by the government's fledgling airborne postal service (in many cases under very hazardous flying conditions) to local offices of the Veterans Administration, the agency designated as the program's paymaster because it was the largest and most heavily automated federal disbursing system then in existence.[21]

Because of statutory restrictions on the funds used to finance the program, 90 percent of the work projects undertaken were limited to the planning and execution of construction projects, all work had to be performed on public property, and no project was supposed to duplicate work normally done by state and local governments.[22] Despite these limitations, a surprisingly wide variety of useful projects were set in motion on exceedingly short notice. All together, a total of one hundred and eighty thousand distinct projects were undertaken. Over two hundred and fifty thousand miles of roads were either built or improved. Approximately sixty thousand public buildings were either repaired or constructed. Almost twenty-three hundred miles of sewer lines were laid or repaired. The program employed thirty thousand workers in swamp-drainage projects to fight malaria, and seventeen thousand jobless coal miners were put to work sealing abandoned coal mines to protect groundwater supplies. Over thirty-seven hundred new playgrounds and two hundred new swimming pools were constructed. Over forty thousand CWA workers were employed in airport construction at both civilian and military facilities.[23]

Funding from other sources was obtained to permit the establishment of nonconstruction work projects for about 10 percent of the program's workforce. Fifty thousand laid-off teachers were employed in special education programs. Adult education classes run by the CWA were attended by eight hundred thousand adults, and sixty-one thousand preschool children attended CWA nursery schools. A nationwide child health study and immunization campaign was staffed by twenty-three thousand nurses, and over seventy thousand people worked in pest eradication campaigns. Employment was provided to fifteen thousand persons with engineering backgrounds in an extensive triangulation and mapping project for the U.S. Coast and Geodetic Survey, and another ten thousand were employed in an aerial mapping project that charted hundreds of U.S. cities. Work for twelve hundred draftsmen was provided by means of an architectural survey of the nation's historic buildings, and three thousand artists were employed in a meticulously organized Public Works of Art Project sponsored by the Treasury Department. Actors were employed to stage dramatic works in hospitals, schools, and libraries. Opera singers toured the Ozarks. CWA orchestras gave free concerts in New York, Philadelphia, Newark, and Los Angeles. The Smithsonian Institution supervised archeological digs in five states staffed by one thousand CWA workers, and eleven thousand CWA workers took part in a Real Property Inventory sponsored by the Department of Commerce. The program's own statistical division provided work for another thirty-five thousand persons, developing the data and documentation needed to improve program administration and collecting census information about labor market conditions and the nation's public relief problems.[24]

All of this was planned, implemented, and completed in less than five months. One historian of New Deal relief efforts has characterized the achievement as "one of the greatest peacetime administrative feats ever completed" in the United States.[25] It demonstrates what can be done when the political will exists to make a program of this type work.

In principle, at least, the task of finding useful work for participants in a jobs program should be easier today than it was in the 1930s. Government agencies now provide a far greater variety of public goods and services than they did in the past, so it should be possible to identify a broader range of goods and services that an expanded public sector workforce could provide.

The real problem lies not so much in imagining useful goods and services that a jobs program could undertake to provide, but in identifying things that a jobs program would be permitted to do in the face of almost certain political opposition from other potential providers of the same goods and services. While both administrators and workers in existing government agencies would probably welcome EAP funding of additional employee slots within their agencies, they would probably oppose plans to have the jobs program itself provide goods and services that had traditionally been provided by their agencies. Private businesses would be even more strongly opposed to the jobs program providing goods or services they were trying to sell.

In the case of the CWA, it was the construction industry that felt its interests most directly affected, and trade associations in the industry were quick to express their objections to the program. Concerned at the "scope of projects" planned by the CWA, the Illinois Builders Institute called an emergency meeting at which it was resolved to seek the program's termination as quickly as possible. The Pittsburgh Builders Exchange complained to a prominent New Dealer that, "General contractors and subcontractors have had little to do in the past three years and then you set up a construction program which continues to leave them on the outside."[26]

It is political opposition of this type, usually expressed as a concern for workers in the effected industries, which tends to confine public employment programs to less productive activities. It is true, of course, that the operations of an EAP jobs program could have a negative effect on industries (and other government agencies) that provide similar goods and services. Enrollment in nonelite private schools must have declined in the United States when free public education was first introduced, and a similar effect would probably be felt by existing child care providers if an EAP jobs program began to offer that service for free or at a very low cost.

This does not mean, however, that the general level of employment in either the private or the regular government sectors of the economy would necessarily decline as a result of "competition" from the jobs program. The portion of household income and tax revenues formerly spent purchasing goods and services that the jobs program provided for free (or at reduced cost) would henceforth be available for purchases of other goods and services. Employment in immediately effected industries and regular government agencies might indeed decline, but it would be just as likely to increase in other industries, while the public's general level of real consumption would increase by an amount equal to the value of the goods and services produced by the jobs program. The net welfare effect of these changes would almost surely be positive, but this is not likely to diminish the political opposition of those whose private interests would be harmed by "competition" from the jobs program.

Moreover, there is good reason to believe that this political opposition would be effective. During the period immediately following the termination of the CWA (and preceding the establishment of the WPA), New Deal relief agencies provided significant support for the development of self-help production both by private cooperatives of unemployed workers[27] and within public work relief programs.[28] In the summer of 1934, for example, a dozen idle factories were leased by the Ohio State Relief Commission to establish a work relief program producing clothing, furniture, and stoves for direct distribution to the poor. Similar programs were established in other states. Perhaps the most interesting of these were programs linked to the government's surplus commodities program. Cotton purchased by the Federal Surplus Relief Corporation (FSRC) was shipped to factories leased by work relief programs where mattresses were produced for distribution to families on relief. Similar plans were formulated for the use of surplus cattle purchased by the FSRC to produce canned beef and shoes. By the fall of 1934, production-for-use, as it was called, accounted for 15 percent of all employment in federally funded work relief programs.[29]

Private business opposition to such activities, however, was immediate and vociferous. Mattress manufacturers were outraged, and shoe manufacturers refused to rent the government the machinery needed to commence production. As Arthur Schlesinger has noted,

> As these programs developed . . . the phrase "production-for-use" began to acquire sinister connotations. The impression grew in business circles that the self-help program was the entering wedge of socialism. The "Ohio Plan" was suspicious enough; and when Upton Sinclair, running for governor in California, envisaged production-for-use by the unemployed as the nucleus for a radical reconstruction of the economy, reaction was vigorous and unequivocal.[30]

As a result of this opposition, the production-for-use movement within New Deal employment programs was essentially ended. Henceforth, the programs were severely restricted both by statute and as a matter of administration policy from engaging in any activities that would directly compete with private enterprises. Similar restrictions, motivated by fears of fiscal substitution, prevented the programs from engaging in activities that were seen as the responsibility of state and local governments.[31]

An EAP jobs program that ventured to provide goods and services in competition with significant business interests would be sure to encounter similar problems. Thus, the task of identifying work that an EAP laborforce could perform is as much political as it is economic. Jobs would have to be found that matched the skills of program participants and produced goods and services that were genuinely useful, but these activities would also have to be sustainable politically, meaning that they could not trench too severely on private interests. If fears of fiscal substitution led to the adoption of regulations that prevented the program from providing goods and services normally supplied by other government agencies, then the field of possible choices would be made even narrower.

This is not to say that this administrative task would be impossible. Faced with similar political constraints and administrative concerns, New Deal employment programs did succeed in creating jobs for a laborforce of several million persons at a time when the overall size of the public sector was much smaller than it is today. Some idea of the range of activities undertaken by the WPA can be obtained from a perusal of table 2.5.[32]

Conceptually, two distinct kinds of employment opportunities would have to be provided in a modern EAP jobs program. The first would consist of relatively permanent positions needed to fill the economy's structural job deficit. The second would consist of relatively short-term jobs needed to fill any cyclical or seasonal employment gaps.

Assuming that fiscal substitution problems could be controlled without prohibiting the assignment of EAP job-holders to regular government agencies, an obvious place to begin in creating permanent EAP positions would be by restoring or expanding traditional government services. The number of jobs that could be created in this fashion would be considerable. It has been estimated, for example, that a 10 to 15 percent increase in low-skilled public sector employment would have been necessary in 1972 just to restore government services to their 1960 level in the cities of Oakland and San Francisco.[33] A 25 percent increase in the size of the public sector laborforce providing traditional government services would have involved the creation of about four million new full-time jobs between 1977 and 1986, over half the total I have estimated would be needed to employ the entire EAP laborforce.

Jobs could also be created, of course, by expanding government services in new directions. Among the new services that an EAP jobs program could either fund or provide directly, child care would probably be the most widely accepted and relatively uncontroversial priority. Between two and three million child care slots would be needed just to accommodate the preschool age children of former AFDC parents participating in the program.[34] Nationally, there are over eight million children under five years of age with mothers in the laborforce. Only about 23 percent of these mothers are now able to place their preschool age children in organized child care facilities. There are, in addition, another eighteen million children between the ages of five and fourteen with mothers in the laborforce. A substantial number of these children (4.5 million) are not in school and need full-day care on a year-round basis. Even those who are attending school need afternoon care when school is in session and full-day care during that portion of the work year when school is not in session, as well as on school days when they are home sick and their parents have to work.[35]

An enormous unmet need exists in this area, which an EAP jobs program could satisfy while creating several million new jobs. In addition, the program could fund expanded school support services and special services for the elderly and the disabled. Job-training and sheltered-workshop programs within the program would also provide work for substantial numbers of program participants. These activities, in conjunction with the restoration of traditional government services that have been reduced in budget-cutting efforts over the past fifteen years, could probably provide work for the entire EAP laborforce.

There are plenty of other unmet needs, though, that could compete with these for attention—the unmet needs of individuals and families for affordable housing, the need to restore and modernize the nation's physical infrastructure, the need to retrofit the nation's existing housing stock with energy-conserving improvements, and the need for resources to undertake a host of environmental preservation projects from trash recycling to public education campaigns.

Some of these undertakings would be more capital-intensive than I have assumed EAP work projects would be, but they also involve the provision of goods for which people would probably be willing to pay something out of nonprogram funds. Low-income housing provides a good example of this. Unemployment rates are particularly high among youthful workers in inner-city neighborhoods where the housing stock is badly deteriorated. Housing rehabilitation and construction work in such neighborhoods could provide a very large number of jobs in which youthful workers would learn valuable skills. Productivity levels would be low at first, because of the low initial skill levels of the workforce, but they would improve over time. Efforts to minimize labor costs would not in any case be a major concern, because the program's objective would not be to build housing at the lowest possible cost, but to maximize the productivity of the program's workforce. Since the labor cost of the construction work along with a substantial share of the cost of construction materials would already be covered by the program budget, the net uncovered cost of the housing would be very low. Such housing could be made available to low-income families at affordable rents without any public subsidy beyond that already provided by the jobs program.

Housing construction, infrastructure rebuilding, energy conservation, and environmental protection projects would also be well suited to meet the needs of cyclically and seasonally unemployed workers, because such projects could be "stock-piled" for implementation when needed to provide EAP jobs. The bureaucratic problems associated with the administration of rapidly expanding and contracting short-term work projects would be substantial, but more varied projects could be undertaken because of the relatively high average skill levels of seasonally and cyclically unemployed workers. Projects of this type furnished the greatest number of jobs in New Deal employment programs, and there is no reason to doubt the current ability of government agencies and community groups to develop a sufficiently long "wish list" of such projects to keep seasonally and cyclically unemployed EAP job-holders usefully employed.

The possibilities for devising genuinely useful work projects would be further expanded if the projects were allowed to benefit private parties. New Deal work projects were generally limited to public property, but this was not universally the case. In 1935 and 1936 my father worked as a foreman in a Civilian Conservation Corps (CCC) camp in rural Iowa that engaged in soil conservation work on private property. A CCC field engineer would visit farms and walk the land with the owner, discussing what conservation measures were needed and which ones the CCC could perform. These included the erection of small check dams made out of fencing material and debris, the construction of larger dams of reinforced concrete, the digging of erosion flumes (the much-maligned but nonetheless quite functional "ditch"), the terracing of hillsides, and the planting of trees. The property-owners had to provide construction materials or pay the CCC for any it provided. No charge was made for CCC labor and the farmer was not involved in supervising the actual work (which was performed by work crews of twenty-five to thirty CCC enrollees supervised by foremen employed by the Soil Conservation Service of the Department of Agriculture). Any necessary design work was also done by Soil Conservation Service engineers.

The installation of energy-conserving improvements to private property could easily be undertaken using this model, but the possibilities would be virtually limitless if the program were to be conceived, in part, as a program for providing in-kind tax rebates to the public. As long as fair methods of distributing the benefits were devised, the services would not even have to be confined to quasi-public goods.

Creating enough jobs to keep EAP participants productively employed would undoubtedly be easier if the political constraints I have identified as likely to restrict the activities of such a program could be overcome. Even with these constraints, however, society's needs are sufficiently elastic for there to be no shortage of genuinely useful work for an EAP jobs program to perform. What would be needed is a realization of the possibilities opened up by such a program. It would transform unemployment from a private curse into a public opportunity. To waste that opportunity with a poor selection of work projects would be both economically irrational and socially irresponsible.

MAINTAINING WORKER DISCIPLINE

Another difficulty that administrators of an EAP jobs program would face is the task of maintaining good morale and discipline in the program's workforce. Since EAP jobs would be guaranteed, there would seem to be little incentive for participants to exert any but the most nominal effort in the performance of their duties. The Chinese call this the "iron rice bowl" syndrome, a tendency for workers to develop slack work habits when they know that they cannot be dismissed for poor performance. They develop poor discipline because they know that their "rice bowls" cannot be broken.

In formulating a strategy to combat this problem, it is important to distinguish between the right to employment, as I have been using the term, and the right to retain a particular job. When legal scholars in the United States discuss the right to employment, it is usually the latter concept that they have in mind rather than the one that is the subject of this book. The focus of their commentary is the erosion that has occurred during the twentieth century in the "employment at will" doctrine. Under this doctrine, employers are presumed to have the right to dismiss an employee at any time, with or without cause, unless that right has been expressly limited in an employment contract. Since the 1930s, however, the employment at will doctrine has been significantly circumscribed, first by statute and more recently by a growing receptivity on the part of courts to hear and heed opposing common law or constitutional doctrines.[36] This is what most legal scholars mean when they speak of an expanding right to employment in the United States.

My usage of the term is different. Indeed, as I have defined the right to employment it is equally compatible with a legal system that recognizes the employment at will doctrine and one that restricts it. The analysis contained in this book simply does not address the issue of whether the right of employers to dismiss their employees should be limited, but rather the obligation of society to ensure adequate employment opportunities for all job-seekers.

Interestingly, the importance of distinguishing between the right to employment and the right to retain a particular job is illustrated by recent developments in employment law in both the United States and the Soviet Union. The legal protections afforded workers against the threat of unjust dismissal have been increasing in the United States since the 1930s. In recognition of this trend, it is possible to say that something like a property right in one's job is gradually coming to be recognized in this country. On the other hand, this trend has been accompanied by an erosion of the right to employment, as measured by prevailing unemployment rates or by the willingness of the government to take concerted action to secure the right. Indeed, the recent evolution of common law doctrines restricting at will dismissals may be interpreted, in part, as a reaction to the simultaneous erosion of the right to employment. It is certainly hard to imagine these new doctrines developing so quickly if the personal consequences of being fired from a job were not as devastating as they have become.

It is also important to distinguish between the right to employment and the right to retain a particular job in characterizing recent reforms in Soviet employment law. In the American press these reforms are frequently characterized as a repudiation of the legal protections afforded the right to employment in the Soviet Union, but this characterization is only partly accurate. The quasi-property right that Soviet workers have hitherto had in particular jobs is indeed being weakened, but this is not necessarily true of their right to employment as I have defined the term. The changes being introduced will make it easier for Soviet enterprises to dismiss redundant or nonperforming employees, but substantial safeguards still exist to ensure that such workers will be able to find new jobs. Most important, unemployment rates in the Soviet Union are probably in the 1 to 2 percent range consistent with frictional factors alone.[37] Thus, what the reforms really involve, at least so far, is a restriction of the right to retain a particular job, without significantly lessening the right to employment.[38]

Understanding the distinction between the right to employment and the right to retain a particular job is crucial for making a proper assessment of the problem of maintaining worker discipline in an EAP jobs program. In particular, it is important to understand that the program could secure the right to employment without guaranteeing participants a right to keep a particular job regardless of their performance. Indeed, supervisory standards could and should be as strict as those applied to workers employed through the regular labor market. Program participants should not expect to be paid for work missed without proper cause, and they should know that consistent absenteeism or poor performance will result in dismissal from a particular position. The difference would be that another job would be made available to such persons, though not necessarily one that was equally desirable. Persistent unsatisfactory performance should lead to demotion. At the bottom of the barrel would be jobs requiring purely routine casual labor in which wages could be paid on a per diem or piecework basis.

At the same time, it is important to remember that positive as well as negative reinforcements are important in developing good worker morale and discipline. Indeed, only experience can demonstrate what mix of positive and negative sanctions is likely to work best with any particular category of employees. It should not be assumed that the threat of dismissal from a position for unsatisfactory performance will necessarily work better than the promise of promotion for good performance. EAP job-holders who perform well in their work could and should be rewarded in conventional ways—with praise, with positive performance evaluations, with offers of more desirable jobs, with promotions to more responsible positions, and with regular wage increases.

Special efforts should also be made to be sensitive to the underlying causes of persistent performance problems on the part of individual workers. The root of the problem may be alcoholism, a family crisis, a nervous disorder, or other such phenomena. An EAP jobs program would employ many people with significant personal problems, and a strategy would have to be developed for responding to their needs. In doing this, it should be remembered that whatever the cause of the unsatisfactory work performance, its social cost is significant. Efforts to help workers overcome their personal problems are economically as well as morally justified. It is simply good personnel management.

For example, instead of organizing "bottom-of-the-barrel" assignments as "penalty" work, these should probably be organized along the lines of a sheltered workshop, with special counseling and treatment made available to help workers become more reliably functional and productive. An EAP jobs program could be both tough in enforcing performance standards, when that is needed, and humane in responding to the personal problems that prevent many workers from performing satisfactorily.

CHAPTER 6

Political Problems

THUS FAR I have drawn encouraging conclusions regarding both the fiscal feasibility of an EAP jobs program and its desirability as a policy response to the problems of poverty and unemployment in the United States. I have further argued that neither the economic side effects nor the administrative problems likely to be associated with such a program offer a convincing case against its deployment. Indeed, my analysis of the indirect effects of an EAP jobs program and of the administrative opportunities it would present has suggested further grounds for favoring the idea. Why then has a policy of providing employment assurance never been tried in the United States?

In fact, substantial support did exist for such an initiative during the New Deal era in this country, and two major efforts have been made since then to enact statutory schemes that would have effectively secured the right to employment.[1] None of these initiatives were successful, and a brief review of their history can tell us a great deal about the political barriers that stand in the way of programs designed to provide employment assurance in the United States.

OPPOSITION TO NEW DEAL EMPLOYMENT PROGRAMS

The history of New Deal employment programs provides many examples of the kind of political conflicts that beset proposals to use public sector jobs to fight unemployment and poverty. The pattern these conflicts take is perhaps best illustrated by the brief and politically turbulent history of the Civil Works Administration (CWA). Indeed, the program provides a paradigm for subsequent political conflict in this area.

The CWA was the most ambitious of the New Deal's major public employment programs. It not only employed the largest workforce,[2] it paid the highest wages,[3] and was the only major New Deal jobs program that did not require applicants to pass a means test in order to be declared eligible for employment.[4] It did not oppose the unionization of its workforce, hired skilled workers through union hiring halls, and engaged in collective bargaining with employee organizations.[5] Of all the public employment programs established during the New Deal period, it came the closest to providing the unemployed with "real jobs for real wages."

Harry Hopkins, who directed both the CWA and the WPA, wrote of the program in retrospect:

> I believe CWA will stand out, even when WPA has become past history, like a precocious child in a family of slower-going but more substantial children. For its special quality of having come and gone so quickly, yet having let loose great forces, both economic and spiritual, it shares certain of the memorable qualities of special events.[6]

The establishment of the CWA was a particularly bold gesture, even for the New Deal. It took an extraordinary conjunction of political factors to make it possible and it is worth noting these in order to appreciate how much more difficult it would be to undertake such an initiative in normal times.

Following a small surge in business activity that developed in the early summer after President Roosevelt's March 1933 inauguration, production again resumed the downward spiral that had ravaged the economy since 1929. By fall, unemployment rates were again rising and the view was widely accepted within the Roosevelt administration that a quick dose of fiscal "pump priming" was needed. A large-scale program of conventional (that is, privately contracted) public works spending had just been authorized under the National Industrial Recovery Act (NIRA), but the agency established to spend the funds, the Public Works Administration (PWA), had been delayed by legal and other problems from beginning its projects.[7]

In the meantime, political unrest among the unemployed was growing and was assuming more radical political forms, while public confidence in the business community's economic leadership had reached its nadir.[8] Even among strong supporters of capitalism, the general political and intellectual climate favored a degree of innovation in tackling the nation's economic problems that was, by conventional standards, quite radical. An article by John Maynard Keynes that appeared in the *Yale Review* during the summer of 1933 was symptomatic of the mood of the moment.

> The decadent international but individualist capitalism, in the hands of which we found ourselves after the war, is not a success. It is not intelligent, it is not beautiful, it is not just, it is not virtuous and it doesn't deliver the goods. In short, we dislike it, and we are beginning to despise it. . . . I spend my time half vainly, but also, I must admit, half successfully in trying to persuade my countrymen that the nation as a whole will assuredly be richer if unemployed men and machines are used to build much needed houses than if they are supported in idleness. . . . If I had the power to-day, I should most deliberately set out to endow our capital cities with all the appurtenances of art and civilization on the highest standards of which the citizens of each were individ-

ually capable, convinced that what I could create, I could afford and believing that money thus spent not only would be better than any dole but would make unnecessary any dole. For with what we have spent on the dole in England since the war we could have made our cities the greatest works of man in the world.[9]

It was in this context that the staff of the Federal Emergency Relief Administration (FERA)[10] under the leadership of Harry Hopkins proposed the establishment of a massive, federally administered jobs program as a substitute for the locally administered work relief programs that had hitherto been the primary vehicle for delivering public assistance to the unemployed. Aubrey Williams, Hopkins' chief assistant, expressed the trajectory of their thinking in an October 1933 memo. "Relief as such should be abolished," he wrote. Instead, the unemployed should be offered real jobs paying good daily wages, doing truly useful work that suited their individual skills. Their employment should not be conditioned on submission to a means test and their earnings should not be limited to a relief budget. The goal should be to provide the unemployed with quality employment of the sort normally associated with contracted public works, but to do it at lower cost and with less bureaucratic delay by having the federal government act as its own contractor, and by selecting projects that were less elaborate and more labor-intensive than conventional public works.[11]

A proposal to establish such a program was made by Hopkins to President Roosevelt at a luncheon meeting on 2 November 1933. Congress was in recess at the time, but the president was in the unusual position of having the money necessary to launch such a program in hand. Title 2 of the NIRA was worded broadly enough to allow the diversion of funds intended for the PWA to public works projects operated by force account, that is, with the federal government undertaking the work itself. Much to Hopkins' surprise, Roosevelt approved his proposal on the spot, giving him the go-ahead to employ four million persons through the winter, using $400 million in funds diverted from the PWA. A week later the CWA was formally established by executive order with Hopkins at its head.[12]

The exceptional political climate that existed in the fall of 1933, combined with Roosevelt's extraordinary discretionary control over NIRA funds, made such an experiment possible. It did not, however, make it sustainable. From the very beginning Hopkins knew that the CWA was destined for a short life. At a 6 December 1933 staff meeting, before the program was even a month old, Hopkins concluded that, "It is humanly impossible for anybody to inject any chance of permanence in this thing. If we get action from Congress right away, it will be on a basis of an emergency proposition which will see us through this winter."[13] Hopkins' political assessment was accurate. As it turned out, he could not even win the president's support for the program's continuation.

The forces that arrayed themselves in opposition to the CWA were formidable. First, there was opposition from within the Roosevelt administration because of the program's cost and because of fears that it would become politically entrenched if it were allowed to continue. This opposition was led by Roosevelt's fiscally conservative Budget Director, Lewis Douglas. Douglas's point of view can be surmised from the fact that as a congressman he had criticized President Hoover for being a spendthrift. Unhappy with the direction the New Deal was taking, he later left the administration and began denouncing the similarity between "Franklin Roosevelt's fiscal policies and those of the Soviet Union." Douglas was particularly adamant in his opposition to employment programs, since they accounted for the largest share of new government spending. He believed that direct relief was preferable to work relief because it was cheaper, and he had opposed the establishment of both the Civilian Conservation Corps (CCC) and the PWA in the spring of 1933. Persistent in pressing his views, Douglas became the voice within the administration of business leaders and conservative southern Democrats who opposed continuation of the CWA.[14]

In a 30 December 1933 memo to the president concerning the administration's overall fiscal policy, Douglas made a "last plea" that additional government spending be limited to direct relief and warned that the "credit of the Government" would not be able to support even the level of borrowing already required by existing authorizations. In memos written the following month, Douglas argued specifically and forcefully for the termination of the CWA. To buttress his position, he suggested that if the program were not ended quickly, it might become politically impossible to end it at all. Workers employed by the CWA would become accustomed to public employment, and the more their sense of entitlement to such jobs grew, the more difficult it would be to force them off the public payroll.[15]

Outside the administration, criticism of the CWA focused on allegations of mismanagement and corruption. There were, of course, some instances of both. No program as large as the CWA, as quickly implemented, and as decentralized in its day-to-day operations could be entirely free of such problems. In point of fact, however, such problems appear to have been surprisingly limited in scope. The West Point engineer assigned by the War Department to study the CWA was effusive in his praise of its administration,[16] and the number of criminal cases arising from the operations of the program was very small.[17]

In assessing the extent and importance of these problems it is essential to distinguish between their actual dimensions and their political impact.

There are no objective standards for judging how much incompetence and corruption is tolerable in the administration of a government program, nor any rules for deciding whether the appropriate response to such deficiencies is to continue existing efforts to curb the problem, to reform the program, to replace it, or to terminate it. Relatively extensive profiteering and peculation may be tolerated in a politically popular program, but even minor irregularities in the administration of a controversial one can attract extensive public attention and give rise to concerted calls for its termination.

Such was the fate of the CWA. Hopkins and his staff were themselves unwitting accomplices in this process because they were quick to publicize any irregularities that they uncovered. "I may have made a mistake in kicking a lot of this stuff outdoors," he told Congress, "but I don't like it when people . . . finagle around the back door."[18]

A second group that was active in publicizing alleged program irregularities were politicians, public officials, and private citizens who felt aggrieved at their failure to gain a larger share of pork barrel benefits. Democrats in particular were angered by Hopkins' refusal to allow the program to be used as an instrument of political patronage. As one of the CWA's field representatives commented, "Politicians did not especially mind turning relief over to a group of citizens, for they felt there was nothing but grief in that job. However, it drove the politicians wild to find themselves without anything to say about who was going to get a job on public work."[19]

It was dissatisfaction of this sort that resulted in the most widely publicized case of alleged CWA corruption. Ray Branion, an independent Republican who served briefly as the California state administrator of the CWA, was indicted for corruption, along with Pierce Williams, the CWA field representative for the region and a key Hopkins aide. The U.S. attorney who obtained the indictment was a Democrat who had unsuccessfully sought Branion's job with the support of U.S. Senator William G. McAdoo. (In objecting to Branion's appointment, McAdoo had earlier told Williams that he had been personally instrumental in including the provision in FERA's enabling legislation that authorized the appointment of state relief administrators in order to increase the number of political appointments made available to the Democrats.) The indictment was groundless and it was eventually dismissed, but not before severe political damage had been done to the program.[20]

The strongest critics of the CWA, though, came from the business community. I have already noted the concerted opposition of the construction industry to the program,[21] but employers in general protested that the CWA was having a deleterious effect on the labor market. With official unemployment rates close to 25 percent, the program provided work for only about a third of the unemployed, paid weekly (though not hourly) wages well below the national average, and generally offered only hard outside work in winter weather. Still the CWA was viewed by employers as providing too much job security, too lax a working environment, and too high a level of earnings. The California Farm Bureau Federation complained that CWA wages were higher than those that prevailed in the industry even before the Depression and that they were "causing labor to leave essential work on farms for more lucrative civil works jobs." Industrialists in the Northeast protested that they were losing labor because CWA rates were higher than those mandated by voluntary NRA codes.[22]

It was in the South, though, that this criticism was most vehemently expressed. The purely economic concerns of the region's low-wage employers was reinforced by racist resentment of the program's nondiscriminatory hiring and wage policies. A du Pont vice president and family member wrote that, "Five negroes on my place in South Carolina refused work this spring, after I had taken care of them and given them house rent free and work for three years during bad times, saying they had easy jobs with the Government. . . . A cook on my houseboat at Fort Myer quit because the Government was paying him a dollar an hour as a painter." A North Carolina landlord put it more bluntly: "You can't hire a nigger to do anything for you. . . . High wages is ruinin' 'em." In a letter to the president criticizing the CWA, Georgia Governor Eugene Talmadge enclosed a letter from a local farmer, who complained: "I wouldn't plow nobody's mule from sunrise to sunset for 50 cents per day when I could get $1.30 for pretending to work on a DITCH."[23]

More sophisticated corporate leaders and national business organizations like the U.S. Chamber of Commerce focused their criticism on issues they believed would have greater resonance with the public, namely, the high cost of the CWA and the threat it posed of higher taxes and increased federal power. Most business leaders supported the dole over work relief (because it was cheaper), favored the return of relief programs to local control, and argued for strict means testing in the distribution of all public relief. On this issue, even liberal business leaders broke with the New Deal. Robert E. Wood, the politically liberal chief executive of Sears Roebuck, reflected the sentiments of this sector of the business community in a June 1934 letter to Secretary of Agriculture Henry Wallace. The New Deal's public relief policy, he wrote, was its "one serious mistake." He explained his position as follows: "While it is probably true that we cannot allow everyone to starve (although I personally disagree with this philosophy and the philosophy of the city social worker), we should tighten up relief all along the line, and if relief is to be given it must be on a bare subsistence allowance."[24]

Does this litany of opposition to the CWA mean that it was unpopular with the public at large? To the contrary, there is good reason to believe that the CWA was exceptionally popular. This was particularly true with regard to the people who got jobs on the program. A FERA field investigator wrote to Hopkins from Iowa at the end of the program's first week of operations: "And did they want work? In Sioux City they actually had fist fights over shovels!" A CWA administrator reported: "It was pathetic to watch some of the reactions. I saw a few cases leave the office actually weeping for sheer happiness."[25]

The program was much preferred by the unemployed to traditional forms of work relief.[26] It was also preferred over direct relief. As a *Fortune* magazine report published in October 1934 concluded, men and women on relief "do not like the dole. They are almost unanimous in demanding *work*."[27] Nine million people applied for the two million positions that the CWA made available for persons not on relief.[28] The mayor of Chelsea, Massachusetts, wrote to Hopkins in January 1934 complaining that the city's allocation of 155 CWA jobs was totally inadequate. He warned that two thousand unsuccessful applicants were congregating in City Hall and that "a spark might change them into a mob." He went on:

> I believe that the Federal Government, once having acknowledged its responsibility by giving jobs merely for the sake of a job, must now put every unemployed man to work doing the most useful task that can be found for him. . . .
> If some such remedial measure is not immediately adopted I make bold to predict fundamental and sweeping changes in the structure of our government before the end of the present year.[29]

Social workers expressed concern that enrollees in the program were "beginning to regard CWA as their due, that the Government actually owes it to them. And they want more."[30]

The political problem the CWA faced was not that it was unpopular, but that it was too popular. Douglas was probably not exaggerating when he warned Roosevelt that if the program were not ended quickly, it might be impossible to end it ever. The interests that Douglas represented sensed the danger, and even in the midst of the worst unemployment crisis in the nation's history, they exercised enough political power to control the program's fate.

In the face of the politically potent opposition mobilized against the CWA, and because of his own responsiveness to Douglas's arguments, President Roosevelt decided not to seek the program's continuation.[31] The CWA workweek was reduced beginning 18 January and demobilization officially began on 15 February. By early April, the program's payroll had been reduced to less than one hundred thousand workers.[32]

The strength and political effectiveness of the opposition the CWA inspired is paradigmatic of the political problems faced by other New Deal employment programs. Throughout the 1930s political support for such programs was strong enough at least partially to overcome this opposition, but not strong enough to sustain a program as expansive as the CWA. The more modest WPA probably marked the outer bounds of what was politically feasible.

THE EMPLOYMENT ACT OF 1946

Despite this political opposition, there was significant ongoing support within the Roosevelt administration for the long-term goal of using programs like the CWA eventually to provide employment assurance to the nation's laborforce. That intention was made explicit in the recommendations of the Committee on Economic Security,[33] but an even stronger statement of the policy is found in the 1943 report of the National Resources Planning Board (NRPB).

This very detailed eight-hundred-page report was prepared at President Roosevelt's request to correlate "plans and programs under consideration . . . for post-war full employment, security, and building America."[34] As part of the elaborately detailed plan formulated by the NRPB, it was expressly proposed that the federal government guarantee the right to employment.[35] The strategy contemplated for achieving this goal was similar to the one outlined by the Committee on Economic Security in 1935. The NRPB proposed that:

> To guarantee the right to a job, activities in the provision of physical facilities and service activities should be supplemented by:
>
> (1) Formal acceptance by the Federal Government of responsibility for insuring jobs at decent pay to all those able to work regardless of whether or not they can pass a means test.
>
> (2) The preparation of plans and programs, in addition to those recommended [in the section of this report dealing with] Public Works, for all kinds of socially useful work other than construction, arranged according to the variety of abilities and location of persons seeking employment.
>
> (3) Expansion of the functions of the [U.S.] Employment Service, strengthening its personnel to the end that it may operate as the key mechanism in referring unemployed workers to jobs, whether public or private.
>
> (4) Establishment of a permanent "Work Administration" under an appropriate Federal agency to administer the provision of jobs of socially desirable work for the otherwise unemployed.[36]

Support for this vision of the welfare state was by no means universal within the Roosevelt administration and the president's own attitude seems to have been driven largely by pragmatic considerations, as his dual role in first launching and then scuttling the CWA demonstrates.

Early in 1944, however, there were strong indications that he intended to undertake a major political initiative in this area. The president used his 1944 State of the Union message to challenge Congress to give effect to an "Economic Bill of Rights," which was clearly based on the recommendations of the NRPB.[37]

One of the distinctive features of this proposed "bill of rights" was the balance it struck between (1) the right of every person to be self-supporting (whether as a wage laborer, farmer, or business proprietor) and (2) a series of entitlements whose realization would require a significant expansion in the production of public goods and services and in the provision of cash and in-kind transfer payments (for instance, guarantees of decent housing, adequate medical care, a good education, and economic security in the face of disability, old age, and unemployment).[38]

In the more specific proposals advanced by the NRPB a year earlier, these two categories of economic rights were functionally linked. It was through the production of new public goods and services—partly by means of private contracting, partly by the growth of regular government agencies, and partly by the reestablishment of government employment programs like the WPA—that full employment was seen as achievable.[39] In contrast, Roosevelt's speech contained no specific plans for realizing the rights he identified. In fact, he expressly foreswore any intention of proposing any such plans, asserting that it was the responsibility of Congress to do that.[40]

It is difficult to know what Roosevelt's intentions were in leaving to Congress the task of formulating plans for the implementation of his proposal. An indication of the political prospects of this strategy can be seen in the fact that Congress had killed the NRPB in an appropriations bill three months after receiving its report and seven months before the president's speech.[41] In any case, whatever his long-term intentions may have been, Roosevelt was as good as his word and played virtually no role in subsequent efforts to draft a full employment bill and to mobilize public support for its passage.[42]

A bill designed to secure the right to employment was drafted, however, at the initiative of Senator James Murray (D–Montana).[43] Significantly, it did not adopt the NRPB strategy for the achievement of full employment, but instead called for the adoption of a sufficiently expansive fiscal policy to ensure the availability of private sector jobs for everyone seeking work.

This shift in strategy is significant. It reflected the growing ascendancy of Keynesian economists over their institutionalist counterparts in the formation of liberal social welfare policy in the late New Deal period. The NRPB's report, with its emphasis on economic planning and structural economic reforms, was the last hurrah of the New Deal institutionalists.

Postwar Keynesianism promised full employment without the need to tamper with the microeconomic structure of the economy. This approach was clearly more acceptable to established interests than the program suggested by the NRPB, and this may have played a roll in Senator Murray's decision to adopt it. At the same time, though, there can be little doubt that the growing influence of Keynesianism among U.S. liberals reflected a significant shift to the right in their thinking.

Still, while this approach was clearly less threatening to business interests than a program of direct job creation would have been, it was still bitterly opposed by the business community. Among the most effective lobbying efforts were those organized by the National Association of Manufacturers, the U.S. Chamber of Commerce, the American Farm Bureau Federation (which represented the interests of large growers), and the Committee for Constitutional Government (a citizens' lobby that supported a variety of conservative causes, including a constitutional limitation on income, inheritance, and gift taxes). Since the Murray bill did not propose to use direct hiring by the federal government to achieve full employment, the arguments employed by opponents of the bill raised only a subset of the issues that had proved effective in efforts to end or limit programs like the CWA and the WPA. The most frequently repeated arguments were (1) that full employment and political freedom were incompatible (because of the increase in government power necessary to achieve full employment), (2) that the government paternalism mandated by the bill would kill economic initiative, (3) that deficit spending made necessary by the bill would undermine business confidence, (4) that efforts by the government to base its spending decisions on economic forecasts and planning would prove either futile or harmful, and (5) that full employment would cause inflation.[44]

The interest groups that supported the Murray bill included the National Farmers Union (which represented the interests of small farmers), the Union for Democratic Action (a liberal citizens' lobby), both the AFL and the CIO, the NAACP, the American Veterans Committee, the YWCA, the National Catholic Welfare Conference, the National Council of Jewish Women, and the National Lawyers Guild. The National Farmers Union played an especially important role in first eliciting congressional interest in full employment legislation and the Union for Democratic Action led the effort to mobilize popular support for the Murray bill after it was introduced.[45]

It is important to note, however, that support for the Murray bill was not unqualified even within these groups. Most important in this respect was the attitude of organized labor, because the AFL and the CIO had more political "throw-weight" than any of the other groups within the coalition. Both labor federations did support the bill, the CIO more strongly than the AFL, but their support was relatively slow in coming and was never unreservedly enthusiastic. There was concern in both organizations that the Murray bill was "pie in the sky" legislation that would distract attention from issues—such as unemployment compensation, minimum wages, and the continuation of the Fair Employment Practices Commission—that were of greater immediate concern to the trade union movement. It was not until the late summer and early fall of 1945 that the AFL and the CIO began to publicize their support for the Murray bill and they did so in a manner that emphasized that it comprised only one element in their respective legislative agendas.[46]

Support for the bill tended to be more spirited within the rank and file of the labor movement, and public opinion polls conducted at the time suggest that there was in fact broad popular support for the idea that the federal government should assume responsibility for assuring full employment. As previously noted, even the Republican presidential candidate in 1944 supported direct job creation by the government to achieve full employment.[47]

The widespread public support that existed for the idea of providing employment assurance was never effectively mobilized in support of the Murray bill. Most people did not even know that such a bill was being considered. For example, a poll conducted in a congressional district in Chicago in July 1945 (before the AFL and the CIO had begun to publicize their support for the bill) found that 69 percent of the respondents were totally unaware of "any bill before Congress that will plan for enough jobs for everyone after the war." Only 8 percent of the respondents had heard that such a bill was under consideration and had a correct idea of what it was about. When asked to respond to a hypothetical bill with provisions similar to those contained in the Murray bill, however, 83 percent of the respondents said they would support such a measure.[48]

What this demonstrates is the limited ability of the groups comprising the liberal-labor coalition that supported the Murray bill to transform popular sentiment into effective political pressure. Only the trade union federations had the organizational resources and constituency bases necessary to do this, but they did not throw their full resources into the effort. Even if they had, it must be remembered that only about one-third of the laborforce was unionized at the time. The views of the business community may not have been shared by the public as a whole, but they were politically far more potent.

The political consequences of these factors spelled failure for the effort to secure the right to employment. The Murray bill was not totally defeated, but it was sufficiently weakened by amendment that Senator Robert Taft (R–Ohio), a leader of the fight against the bill, was finally able to declare it innocuous. "I do not think any Republican need fear voting for the bill because of any apprehension that there is a victory in the passage of the full employment bill," he stated "because there is no full employment bill anymore."[49]

In it's original form, the Murray bill had declared that "all Americans able to work and seeking work have the right to useful, remunerative, regular, and full-time employment," and that "it is the policy of the United States to assure the existence at all times of sufficient employment opportunities" to enable them to exercise the right. The means specified for achieving that goal included assistance to "industry, agriculture, labor and state and local governments in achieving continuing full employment," but "to the extent that continuing full employment cannot otherwise be achieved, it is the further responsibility of the Federal Government to provide such volume of Federal investment and expenditure as may be needed to assure continuing full employment."[50] The first published draft of the bill prepared by the staff of the War Contracts Subcommittee was even stronger. It had included a provision that would have automatically appropriated "such sums as may be necessary" to achieve the needed level of federal spending.[51] In its final form, though, the Employment Act of 1946 merely proclaimed that:

> It is the continuing policy and responsibility of the Federal Government to use all practicable means consistent with its needs and obligations and other essential considerations of national policy . . . to coordinate and utilize all its plans, functions, and resources for the purpose of creating and maintaining . . . conditions under which there will be afforded useful employment, for those able, willing, and seeking to work, and to promote maximum employment, production, and purchasing power.[52]

In short, all that survived was a formal commitment to the goal of achieving "maximum employment."

THE FULL EMPLOYMENT AND BALANCED GROWTH ACT OF 1978

The issue of whether the federal government should assume responsibility for the provision of employment assurance remained politically dormant in the United States throughout the 1950s, and, surprisingly, during the early part of the War on Poverty era as well. In the mid 1970s, though, another legislative effort was made to secure the right to employment. The political battle that ensued was in all essential respects a reprise of its predecessor.

The effort formally began in June 1974 when Representative Augustus Hawkins (D–California) introduced a bill that, if it had been adopted, would have established a legally enforceable right to employment in the United States.[53] In this respect, the Hawkins bill promised more than the full employment bill introduced in 1945 by Senator Murray. The reason the Hawkins bill could contain such a provision is because it was based on the strategy for achieving full employment proposed by the Committee on Economic Security in 1935 and by the NRPB in 1943 rather than on the Keynesian strategy adopted by the drafters of the Murray bill. Whereas the Murray bill assumed that full employment could be achieved through a sufficiently expansive fiscal policy, the Hawkins bill provided for the federal government to serve as the employer of last resort for persons unable to obtain employment through the regular labor market.

Senator Hubert Humphrey (D–Minnesota) sponsored an identical bill in the Senate and it was henceforth known as the Humphrey-Hawkins bill. In March 1975 a more fully specified version of the bill was unveiled in response to rapidly rising unemployment rates, but over the next three years it was progressively modified and weakened in an effort to put together a political coalition capable of winning its enactment.[54]

Whereas the original bill would have established a legally enforceable right to employment for all job-seekers regardless of age or disability, the 1978 act merely "declares and establishes as a national goal the fulfillment of the right to full opportunities for useful paid employment at fair rates of compensation of all individuals able, willing, and seeking to work."[55] At the same time, however, this commitment is qualified by joining to it a host of other policy goals, including a reduction in the rate of inflation, the achievement of a balanced federal budget, and the minimization of federal outlays as a share of GNP.[56] It was in fact part of the strategy of opponents of the Humphrey-Hawkins initiative to weaken the bill by adding goals to it.[57]

On the other hand, the 1978 act did establish a time limit for achieving its employment goals. The unemployment rate was supposed to be reduced to 4 percent within five years, and full employment was to be achieved "as soon as practicable" thereafter.[58] Nevertheless, this commitment was toothless because no mandatory measures were enacted for achieving these goals. The spirit of the act is best reflected in the following weasel language:

> It is . . . the purpose of this title to require the President to initiate, as the President deems appropriate, with recommendations to the Congress where necessary, supplementary programs and policies to the extent that the President finds such action necessary to help achieve these goals.[59]

In other words, the 1978 act fell as far short of realizing the goals of the original Hawkins bill as did the 1946 act with reference to the goals of the original Murray bill.

Also as in the 1940s the political failure of this effort to secure the right to employment occurred despite apparently widespread popular support for the idea that the federal government should provide employment assurance. Evidence of this support from public opinion polls is cited in the introduction to this book.[60] Political decision making reflects political power, however, and the intrinsic popularity of a proposal does not necessarily translate into effective political support for its adoption. The liberal-labor coalition that supported the Hawkins initiative was similar to the one that had supported the Murray bill, and it was similarly unsuccessful in mobilizing the kind of popular support that would have been needed for this effort to succeed. The business and other conservative interest groups that had defeated effective full employment legislation in the 1940s once again demonstrated that on this issue they are more than a match for their liberal opponents.[61]

POLITICAL BARRIERS TO THE PROTECTION OF HUMAN RIGHTS

This analysis of the political problems that beset earlier efforts to secure the right to employment in the United States inspires little optimism regarding the political prospects of an EAP initiative. Despite the feasibility and the desirability of adding employment assurance to the list of social welfare benefits provided by the federal government, and despite the broad popular support that seems to exist for the idea, there are powerful political interests that oppose it. More importantly, these interests have consistently demonstrated their capacity to block legislative initiatives in this area.

My analysis of the probable side effects and administrative problems associated with an EAP jobs program suggests reasons for the strength of this opposition. It is not wrongheaded. It is self-interested. It is certainly not surprising that employers in general, and especially low-wage employers, would oppose programs that not only aim to raise wages among low-wage workers, but would also tend to strengthen the bargaining power of workers generally. Business leaders are not likely to admit it publicly, but they do not perceive full employment to be in their interest and will generally oppose measures designed to achieve it. It is also not surprising that the business community would oppose proposals to expand the government's role as a direct provider of goods and services. Such proposals not only threaten specific business interests, they bear the taint of socialism.

Another source of opposition to employment assurance proposals can be found in the biases of neoclassical economic theory. Conservative economists are generally not prepared to admit that active management of the economy is needed to achieve full employment, and their liberal counterparts are generally not prepared to countenance measures for

achieving full employment that extend beyond macroeconomic manipulation. Neither group believes that direct job creation by the government is either necessary or desirable to achieve full employment. Given the influence of neoclassical economic theory on public policy analysis in the United States, it is not surprising that employment assurance proposals have not attracted much scholarly support, or even interest, in recent decades; and without academic support, such proposals are not likely to receive serious political consideration.

The relative ineffectiveness of efforts to mobilize popular support for employment assurance proposals is also understandable. The groups in the population that would most benefit from the introduction of employment assurance—unemployed workers, low-wage workers, poor people generally—are among the politically weakest members of our society. They possess very little direct political influence, and organizations that do try to represent their interests tend to have other constituencies whose concerns demand priority. Trade unions, for example, can generally be counted on to support employment assurance proposals, but since their primary constituency consists of employed workers, support for such proposals will probably take a second seat to other concerns. Civil rights organizations are also likely to direct their primary energy to other issues. As the label identifying these organizations implies, the influence they exercise has been gained primarily in the struggle to defend the civil and political human rights of the populations they represent. They are less well-equipped to fight for the realization of economic and social human rights, and to do so effectively they would have to reorient their work in fundamental ways.

There are understandable reasons, then, for the failure of the United States to secure the right to employment. Groups opposed to the idea exercise substantial political power and benefit from a well-articulated ideology supporting their position. Even though they represent what is probably a minority point of view on the issue, these groups are able to dominate public policy debate. Support for the idea that the government should guarantee the right to employment may be widespread, but it has never been successfully mobilized and therefore it remains politically impotent.

This is not to say that the nation's failure to secure the right to employment is excusable. If access to useful and remunerative work is indeed a human right, then the fact that entrenched political interests have the power to block initiatives to secure that right cannot be regarded as creating a license to accept that outcome. It is a basic principle of international human rights law (as it is of United States constitutional law) that even a democratically elected legislature, representing the perceived in-

terests of a majority of a nation's population, may not properly refuse to recognize the human rights of a disadvantaged minority group.

A white majority cannot properly refuse to protect the human rights of a nonwhite minority, even if the political process from which the majority derives its putative authority is open to both whites and nonwhites on equal terms. Similarly, if unemployed individuals really are entitled to protection of their right to employment, then even a democratically elected legislature may not properly decide that it is unnecessary or inconvenient to take steps to secure the right.

Moreover, before dismissing the right to employment as someone else's concern, human rights advocates should ponder the consequences of a failure to secure the right—the lives lost as a result of the material deprivations and psychological stress attributable to unemployment and the poverty that attends it, the physical and emotional suffering people endure, the social costs communities bear, the damage done to our collective humanity, the amount of this suffering borne by children. In short, human rights advocates should consider whether the consequences of a government's failure to secure the right to employment are any less serious than the consequences that attend violations of key civil and political rights.

A government's failure to secure the right to employment when it has the capacity to do so is a serious human rights offense. It is not a minor matter. Like freedom of conscience and speech, the right to employment is a cornerstone entitlement. To the degree that it is realized, the task of achieving adequate protection for a host of other human rights (including civil and political ones) is eased. If it is denied, the realization of many other human rights becomes virtually impossible.

Human rights advocates have for too long been hesitant to demand the same progress from governments in the protection of economic and social human rights that they expect with respect to the protection of civil and political rights. To be sure, international standards regarding the protection of economic and social human rights are not very demanding, but an obligation at least to strive for their realization is generally acknowledged.[62] Where practical measures actually do exist for securing one of these rights, governments should be held accountable for their failure to adopt them.

Under the terms of the Employment Act of 1946, as amended by the Full Employment and Balanced Growth Act of 1978, the federal government of the United States has expressly acknowledged its obligation to use all practical means to secure the right to employment. If this pledge is being unreasonably disregarded, then the government's nonfeasance should be viewed as a violation of the human rights of the unemployed. Moreover, the violation should be deemed a serious one, because its con-

sequences are both far-reaching and profoundly destructive of the human personality.

I believe the analysis contained in this book demonstrates that the United States does have the capacity to secure the right to employment without unreasonably impinging on other legitimate public policy goals. Indeed, my analysis supports such an initiative on grounds of self-interest alone. If, then, a practical method for securing the right to employment does in fact exist, a strong human rights claim can be made that the government of the United States has a moral obligation (and arguably a legal duty under international human rights law) to secure the right.

It is no longer enough to proclaim the realization of the right to employment to be a long-term goal of public policy in this country. The time has come for the right to be secured in fact. The specific means I have proposed for achieving that end need not be adopted, but some combination of measures that are similarly effective ought to be viewed as morally and legally obligatory, not just pragmatically desirable.

Realistically, of course, significant political change would have to occur in the United States for the right to employment to be secured, and even liberal politicians display little interest in launching such an effort. Among recent major party presidential aspirants, for example, only Jesse Jackson and Paul Simon have sought to identify themselves with this issue.

Interestingly, the different policy proposals advanced by Reverend Jackson and Senator Simon to secure the right to employment illustrate the alternative strategies that I have identified as underlying past attempts to secure the right in the United States. Jackson presidential campaign materials suggested that a major expansion in federal spending for such items as housing, education, health care, job training and child care (financed by a combination of tax increases on the wealthy and reductions in military spending) would be sufficient to achieve full employment.[63] Thus, the Jackson strategy for securing the right to employment is similar to that embodied in Senator Murray's original Full Employment Bill of 1945.

Senator Simon, on the other hand, has proposed a modest version of the strategy embodied in the original Humphrey-Hawkins full employment bill. Specifically, he has proposed that the federal government finance a limited "Guaranteed Job Opportunities Program," which would offer employment in locally administered work projects to all persons eighteen years of age and older who have been out of work for at least five weeks. The jobs would pay only the statutory minimum wage, however, and would provide only thirty-two hours of work per week.[64]

Given the rightward political drift of the nation in recent years, the lack of serious attention being given to proposals such as these is hardly

surprising. If history is any guide, however, the issue will not remain politically dormant forever. At some point in time a new campaign to secure the right to employment is sure to emerge in the United States. The logic that supports such an initiative and the needs it would address are too compelling for the idea to be permanently banished.

In the final analysis, it is simply irrational for a society to allow a sizable segment of its workforce to remain in a condition of involuntary idleness. If we were not accustomed to the situation, and if we were not convinced that it was unavoidable, we would not tolerate it. Additionally, the hardships that the unemployed and their families are forced to endure constitute a grievous assault on human dignity. Thus, while an argument based on self-interest alone can be made on behalf of an initiative to secure the right to employment, that argument is buttressed by a powerful moral claim as well.

If the force of both of these considerations could be driven home to the American people, that is, if both the self-interest and the conscience of the nation could be successfully engaged on behalf of this issue, then it might be possible to transform the broad spontaneous support that already exists for the idea of guaranteeing the right to employment into effective political pressure on behalf of the idea.

Even then it might not be possible to overcome the tradition of political opposition that has stymied past efforts to secure the right to employment. Knowing the political history of these efforts, it is hard to be optimistic on this score. This is hardly an unusual situation, though, in the struggle for human rights, and human rights claims can sometimes catalyze a process of political and social change whose force confounds seemingly reasonable expectations. That is especially true when strong human rights claims are reinforced, as in this case, by equally strong considerations of collective self-interest. Thus, while it would be foolish to overestimate the chances of the United States acting to secure the right to employment in the near future, it would also be a mistake to write off the possibility.

In any case, it is a policy initiative that I am convinced will eventually succeed. After all, given the balance of political power that existed in the United States at the beginning of the twentieth century, it would have seemed equally improbable to expect the modern welfare state to emerge. Major shifts do occasionally occur in the balance of political power in a country, and these shifts can usher in dramatic changes in what is politically conceivable.

Guaranteeing the right of all job-seekers to useful and remunerative employment is an idea of such inherent good sense and such irresistible moral appeal that it cannot be dismissed as nothing more than an echo of the New Deal. It is an idea that is firmly rooted both in American think-

ing about society's responsibilities to its individual members and in evolving international conceptions of human rights. It is an idea of the future, not of the past. At some point in time the political opposition that has hitherto blocked experimentation in this area will surely be overcome. It won't happen all at once, and initial efforts to implement programs such as the one proposed in this book may be disappointingly limited in scope, but eventually the right to employment will be secured in the United States.

Appendix: Sources and Assumptions for Tabular Data

TABLE 2.1

For "Unemployed Persons," see *Employment and Earnings* (monthly), table A–1.

Figures for "AFDC Parents Not In The Laborforce" are estimates based on the number of AFDC adult recipients who were categorized as neither employed, incapacitated, on layoff, or seeking work in two studies of AFDC recipient characteristics, one conducted in 1979 and the other in 1986. The ratio of such adults to the total number of AFDC recipient families at the time of the two studies was used to estimate the number of such adults in other years. The 1979 ratio was used to estimate figures for 1977–81. The 1986 ratio was used to estimate figures beginning with 1982, the year in which the eligibility-restricting Omnibus Budget Reconciliation Act of 1981 took effect. See U.S. Department of Health and Human Services, *AFDC: 1979 Recipient Characteristics Study*, Part 1, *Demographic and Program Statistics* (1982), pp. 12 (table 1), 45 (table 27), 57 (table 37); idem, *Aid to Families with Dependent Children: Characteristics and Financial Circumstances of AFDC Recipients, 1986* (undated), pp. 29 (table 1), 53 (table 22), 56 (table 25); *Social Security Bulletin, Annual Statistical Supplement* (1986), table 204; *Quarterly Public Assistance Statistics* (quarterly), table 1; and U.S. Congress, House of Representatives, Committee on Ways and Means, *Background Material and Data on Programs within the Jurisdiction of the Committee on Ways and Means*, 98th Cong., 2d sess., 1984, WMCP 98–22, p. 311.

Figures for "Discouraged Workers" include persons reported as wanting a job but not seeking work because they think they cannot get a job due either to job market or personal factors. See U.S. Bureau of Labor Statistics, *Handbook of Labor Statistics*, bulletin 2217 (Washington, D.C.: U.S. Government Printing Office, 1985), p. 38 (table 14); and *Employment and Earnings*, Household Data Annual Averages (January 1985–87), table 35.

Figures for "Involuntary Part-Time Workers" include persons at work less than thirty-five hours per week for economic reasons who usually work part-time. See Bureau of Labor Statistics, *Handbook of Labor Statistics*, p. 60 (table 22); and *Employment and Earnings*, Household Data Annual Averages (January 1985–87), table 31.

Figures for the "Official Unemployment Rate" are for the noninstitutional population sixteen years and over. The unemployment rate for this population is slightly lower than the rate for the civilian laborforce reported in tables 1.1 and 1.2. This is because the total adult laborforce includes the nation's resident armed forces, all of whom are employed. See *Employment and Earnings* (monthly), table A–1.

TABLE 2.2

Estimates of the total jobs needed for "Officially Unemployed Persons," "Discouraged Workers," and "AFDC Parents" are all based on the number of additional jobs that would have been needed to reduce the unemployment rate to 2 percent, assuming that 50 percent of all discouraged workers and 90 percent of all AFDC parents not already counted in the laborforce would have joined the laborforce. It was further assumed that all three groups experienced the same rate of frictional unemployment. For data on the number of persons in each of the three groups, see table 2.1. For the reported size of the laborforce, see *Employment and Earnings* (monthly), table A–1. Ninety percent of the jobs provided for AFDC parents were assumed to be full-time. The ratio of full-time to part-time jobs for officially unemployed persons and discouraged workers is based on the proportion of officially unemployed persons looking for full-time as opposed to part-time work. See Bureau of Labor Statistics, *Handbook of Labor Statistics*, p. 24 (table 7); and *Employment and Earnings*, Household Data Annual Averages (January 1985–87), table 7.

Estimates of the total jobs needed for "Involuntary Part-Time Workers" are based on the number of additional jobs that would have been needed for involuntary part-time workers (see table 2.1) if they had taken such jobs in the same proportion that we have assumed for wholly unemployed persons (redefined to include the above-indicated proportions of discouraged workers and AFDC parents).

Figures for the "Official Unemployment Rate" are from table 2.1 above.

TABLE 2.3

The "Average Hourly EAP Wage Rate" for each year is the weighted averages of EAP wage rates for officially unemployed persons and all other program participants, based on estimates of the total number of hours each group would have worked in EAP jobs (assuming the distribution of jobs indicated in table 2.2 and counting all part-time jobs as half-time positions).

Estimates of the average wage rate for "Officially Unemployed Persons" equal 79 percent of the average hourly earnings of production or nonsupervisory workers on private nonagricultural payrolls. See Bureau of Labor Statistics, *Handbook of Labor Statistics*, p. 194 (table 75); and *Employment and Earnings*, Household Data Annual Averages (January 1985–87), table 65.

Estimates of the average wage rate for "All Other Program Participants" equal the median weekly earnings of part-time wage and salary workers divided by the average weekly hours of persons at work one to thirty-four hours. For data on average weekly hours, see *Employment and Earnings* (January 1978–83), table 33, and (January 1984–87), table 31. For data on median weekly earnings, see ibid., (January 1986–87), tables 54, 55; and *Employment and Earnings*, Quarterly Household Data, tables reporting median weekly earnings of full-time and part-time wage and salary workers by selected characteristics. Hourly wages for 1977 and 1978 are estimates based on the average ratio of the hourly wages calculated for 1979–86 to the average hourly earnings of production or nonsupervisory workers on private nonagricultural payrolls.

For federal statutory minimum wage rates, see *Statistical Abstract of the United States: 1987*, p. 404 (table 684).

TABLE 2.4

All estimates of annual full-time income were calculated by multiplying the wage rates listed in table 2.3 by 2,080 (forty hours times fifty-two weeks).

For "Poverty Thresholds by Household Size," see the Committee on Ways and Means, *Background Material and Data on Programs within the Jurisdiction of the Committee on Ways and Means* (1988), p. 711 (table 1).

TABLE 2.6

Estimates of the "Wages" and "Materials" components of the program's overall "Budgeted Cost" were calculated in the following way: A preliminary wage bill was calculated for the number of jobs listed in table 2.2, paying wages listed in table 2.3. It was assumed that all full-time jobs would pay wages for 2,080 hours per year (40 hours × 52 weeks), and that all part-time jobs would pay wages for 1,040 hours per year (20 hours × 52 weeks). The net additional cost of facilities, tools, and materials was assumed to be one-sixth of this amount (half of the actual expenditures for these items, since half of their cost was assumed to end up as wage and salary payments to private sector employees who would otherwise have to be employed by the EAP jobs program). This total net expenditure for wages and materials was then reallocated between the two entries, with 75 percent of the total listed as wages (the program's "adjusted wage bill") and the other 25 percent listed as materials (the program's total expenditures for facilities, tools, and materials).

Estimates of the "Benefits" component of the program's overall "Budgeted Cost" include the employer's share of Social Security taxes and of health insurance premiums for a workforce of the size indicated by the program's total adjusted wage bill. For Social Security Tax rates, see *Statistical Abstract of the United States: 1987*, p. 348 (table 586). Estimates of health insurance premiums are based on those paid by the government for the Blue Cross/Blue Shield health insurance packages described in the text. It was assumed that all former AFDC parents and all officially unemployed full-time workers with children under eighteen would elect family coverage, and that the balance of the EAP workforce would elect individual coverage. It was further assumed that the program's full-time workforce would choose the "standard" and "high option" plans in equal numbers, while the program's part-time workers would all elect the standard plan. For the proportion of all officially unemployed persons with children under eighteen, see *Employment and Earnings*, Household Data Annual Averages (January 1982), table 61; (January 1984), table 52; (January 1986, 1987), table 50. For the distribution of workers between full-time and part-time jobs, see above, table 2.2. Health insurance premiums were from unpublished data, Office of Personnel Management, Office of Management and the Budget. Data for 1980–82 can be found in U.S. Congress, House of Representatives, Committee on the Post Office and Civil Service, *Review of the Federal Employee Health Benefit Program*, 97th Cong., 2d sess., 15 July 1982, p. 79 (appendix A).

Estimates of "Tax Savings" are based on the following assumptions: (1) that Social Security taxes would have been paid on the program's entire direct wage bill and on half of the amount spent on materials, (2) that federal income taxes would have been paid on the program's direct wage bill at the rate of 7.6 percent, the average rate for taxpayers with adjusted gross incomes equal to the program's average annual wage in 1983, (3) that federal income taxes would have been paid on the program's expenditures for materials at the rate of 14.5 percent, the average rate for all taxpayers in 1983, (4) that state and local income taxes would have been paid on both the program's direct wage bill and expenditures for materials, and that the ratio of these taxes to federal income tax receipts would have equaled 19.1 percent, the ratio of all state and local personal income tax revenue to all federal personal income tax revenue for 1983. See *Statistical Abstract of the United States: 1987*, p. 348 (table 586). For average effective federal income tax rates, see ibid., p. 505 (table 500). For the ratio of state and local tax revenues to federal tax revenues, see ibid., p. 253 (table 432).

TABLE 2.8

All figures include administrative costs, where those are available. All figures except for UI are estimates based on adjustments to the data reported in table 2.7.

Figures for "UI" include all expenditures for unemployment compensation benefits. See the Committee on Ways and Means, *Background Material and Data on Programs within the Jurisdiction of the Committee on Ways and Means* (1984), pp. 228–29 (table 1); and idem, 100th Cong., 1st sess., 1987, WMCP 100–4, p. 325 table 1.

Estimates of "AFDC" expenditures are based on the following considerations: About 8.5 percent of all AFDC families do not include a mother or other adult caretaker in the assistance unit. See the Committee on Ways and Means, *Background Material and Data on Programs within the Jurisdiction of the Committee on Ways and Means* (1987), p. 433 (table 23). These are families of related children whose parents are both either absent from home or deceased. They are either living with a relative other than one of their parents (usually a grandparent) or are wards of the state who have been placed in the foster care system. The average size of this type of assistance unit is only about half that of AFDC families as a whole. See U.S. Department of Health and Human Services, *Recipient Characteristics and Financial Circumstances of AFDC Recipients: 1983* (undated), pp. 36, 38; and idem, *Aid to Families with Dependent Children: Characteristics and Financial Circumstances of AFDC Recipients, 1986* (undated), pp. 32 (table 4), 35 (table 7). Presumably, these families receive about half the average AFDC family benefit, or the equivalent of the average benefit for half as many families (that is, about 4.25 percent of all AFDC families). Another 4.5 percent of all AFDC families (on average) are headed by a parent or other adult caretaker who is incapacitated. Thus, the equivalent of about 8.75 percent of all AFDC households of average size are either headed by an incapacitated caretaker or have no adult caretaker in the assistance unit. Conversely, about 91.25 percent of all such families can be presumed to have an able-bodied adult caretaker present. It has been assumed that this proportion of all AFDC benefits were paid to such families.

Figures for "Other Cash Aid" include expenditures for the following programs:

1. *General Assistance* (GA): General Assistance is funded entirely at the state and local level and eligibility requirements vary greatly. Some jurisdictions provide benefits only for "unemployables." Others provide benefits mostly to employable single adults ineligible for other income maintenance benefits. See U.S. Department of Health and Human Services, *Characteristics*

of General Assistance Programs, 1982, (May 1983). The share of all benefits that go to employable persons and their families is therefore hard to estimate. For purposes of this table, it has been assumed that 50 percent of all benefit payments go to support the families of employable persons. Whether this estimate is high or low is hard to say, but total GA benefit payments averaged less than $1.8 billion per year over the period in question, so the error introduced into our overall calculation is small in either case.

2. *General Assistance to Refugees and Cuban/Haitian Entrants*: This is a federal program that reimburses states for their share of SSI, AFDC and other aid provided to certain categories of refugees. It has been assumed that the same proportion of these funds went to the families of employable persons as to those in the AFDC program, after subtracting SSI reimbursements from the total expenditure figures. This probably understates the amount of aid paid to employable householders, since refugee families were eligible for AFDC payments even if both parents were in the home and neither was sick or unemployed.

3. *Earned Income Tax Credit*: It has been assumed that all benefits went to employable persons.

4. *Emergency Assistance*: Like AFDC, this program provides aid to destitute families with children. It has therefore been assumed that the same percentage went to the families of employable persons as was assumed for the AFDC program.

5. *General Assistance To Indians*: It has been assumed that the same portion of this assistance went to the families of employable persons as was assumed for the AFDC program.

Estimates of "Medicaid" expenditures are based on the assumption that the proportion of all Medicaid benefits going to the families of employable persons equaled the proportion of such benefits made on behalf of AFDC recipients and "others" as opposed to persons who were over sixty-five years old, blind, or disabled. See *Statistical Abstract of the United States: 1984*, p. 388 (table 643); and *Statistical Abstract of the United States: 1987*, p. 359 (table 611).

Figures for "Other Medical Care" include expenditures for the following programs: Maternal and Child Health Services, General Assistance (medical care component), Indian Health Services, Community Health Centers, Medical Assistance to Refugees and Cuban/Haitian Entrants, and Migrant Health Centers. For all of these programs it has been assumed that the same proportion of benefits go to the families of able-bodied persons under age sixty-five as has been assumed for the Medicaid program. This is probably an underestimation because, eligibility for

124 · Appendix

care under these programs is much broader for nondisabled persons under the age of sixty-five than is the case with Medicaid.

Estimates of expenditures for "Food Stamps" are based on the following considerations: During 1982, 8.0 percent of all Food Stamp benefits went to persons living in households headed by someone sixty-five years of age or older. See U.S. Bureau of the Census, *Current Population Reports*, series P–60, no. 141, "Characteristics of Households Receiving Selected Non-Cash Benefits: 1982," pp. 12–13. Cf. *Statistical Abstract of the United States: 1987*, p. 344 (table 580). A 1983 study found that whereas 9.7 percent of all Food Stamp recipients lived in households headed by someone sixty-five years of age or older, only 8.4 percent lived in households that received some ssi benefit payments and were headed by someone less than sixty-five years of age. See U.S. Bureau of the Census, *Current Population Reports*, series P–70, no. 1, "Economic Characteristics of Households in the United States: Third Quarter 1983," p. 24. If we assume that individuals living in nonelderly ssi families received, on average, the same amount of Food Stamp benefits as elderly recipients, then they would have received about 6.9 percent of all Food Stamp benefits in 1982. By combining the 8.0 percent going to persons living in households with an elderly head and the 6.9 percent assumed to be going to the families of disabled workers under the age of sixty-five, we arrive at an estimate of about 15 percent of Food Stamp benefits going to the families of either elderly or disabled householders. It has been assumed that the balance (85 percent) go to the families of able-bodied persons of working age.

Figures for "Other Food Aid" include expenditures for the School Lunch Program (free and reduced-price segments), the Special Supplemental Food Program for Women, Infants & Children (WIC), Special Food Donations, the Temporary Emergency Food Assistance Program, the School Breakfast Program (free and reduced-price segments), the Child Care Food Program, the Summer Food Service Program for Children, the Food Distribution Program for Needy Families, the Special Milk Program (free segment), and the Commodity Supplemental Food Program. Because these programs are all designed to serve low-income families with children, it has been assumed that the same proportion of the assistance goes to the families of able-bodied recipients as was assumed for the AFDC program (that is, 91.25 percent).

Figures for "Housing and Energy Aid" include expenditures for Section 8 Lower-Income Housing Assistance, Low-Rent Public Housing, Section 502 Rural Housing Loans, Section 515 Rural Rental Housing Loans, Section 236 Interest Reduction Payments, Section 235 Home Ownership Assistance for Low-Income Families, Section 521 Rural Rental Assistance, Section 101 Rent Supplements, Section 504 Rural

Housing Repair Loans and Grants, Section 514 Farm Labor Housing Loans, Section 516 Farm Labor Housing Grants, Indian Housing Improvement Grants, Section 523 Rural Self-Help Technical Assistance, Low-Income Energy Assistance, and Weatherization Assistance. Of the 3.5 million households living in public or subsidized housing during the summer of 1983, 31.9 percent were headed by persons sixty-five years of age or older, and 9.8 percent were households that received some SSI benefit payments but were headed by persons less than sixty-five years of age. See U.S. Bureau of the Census, "Economic Characteristics of Households in the United States: Third Quarter 1983," p. 23. Cf. *Statistical Abstract of the United States: 1987*, p. 344 (table 580). It has been assumed that all other households living in such housing (58.3 percent of the total) are headed by able-bodied persons, and that these latter households receive, on average, the same monetary benefits as the other 41.7 percent. It has also been assumed that all other housing and energy aid programs distribute their benefits in similar proportions.

Figures for "Jobs and Training" include all expenditures for jobs and training programs. Figures for "Education Aid" include only those funds spent on the College Work-Study Program, the Vocational Education Work Study Program, and the Headstart Program (the latter because funding for day care, including educational enrichment programing for preschool children, would be included in the budget of the EAP jobs program).

Figures for "Social Services" include 30 percent of Title 20 Social Services expenditures. This is the approximate proportion of all Title 20 funds that were spent for child day care, employment, and training services during 1979. See the Committee on Ways and Means, *Background Material and Data on Programs within the Jurisdiction of the Committee on Ways and Means* (1984), p. 419 (table 5).

TABLE 2.9

Estimates of the funding surplus or deficit contained in the last row of the table are estimates of the surplus or deficit that an EAP jobs program would have experienced if the funds available for reallocation to the program (from the programs listed in table 2.7) had continued to bear the same relationship to total government spending as in 1977 (when total expenditures on the programs listed in table 2.7 equaled 11 percent of all government spending). For data on total government spending, see *Statistical Abstract of the United States: 1987*, p. 249 (table 427); and *Statistical Abstract of the United States: 1988*, p. 257 (table 430).

Notes

Introduction

1. See the Universal Declaration of Human Rights, U.N. Doc. A/811 (1948), Art. 23; the International Covenant on Economic, Social and Cultural Rights, G.A. Res. 2200, 21 U.N. GAOR Supp. (No. 16) at 49, U.N. Doc. A/6316 (1966), arts. 6, 7; the European Social Charter, Europ. T.S. No. 35, 529 U.N.T.S. 89 (1961), art. 1; the Convention Concerning Employment Policy (International Labor Organization Convention No. 122), adopted 15 July 1966, reprinted in International Labor Organization, *International Labour Conventions and Recommendations, 1919–1981* (Geneva: International Labor Office, 1982), pp. 67–68; and the Draft Protocol Additional to the American Convention on Human Rights, Organization of American States, *Annual Report of the Inter-American Commission on Human Rights, 1985–1986* (Washington, D.C.: General Secretariat, Organization of American States, 1986), p. 201, art. 6. For a general discussion of the status of the right to employment in international and metropolitan law, see Jean Mayer, "The Concept of the Right to Work in International Standards and the Legislation of ILO Member States," *International Labour Review* 124 (1985): 228–39.

2. Message to the Congress on the State of the Union (11 January 1944), reprinted in Samuel I. Rosenman, ed., *The Public Papers and Addresses of Franklin D. Roosevelt*, 13 vols. (New York: Harper & Brothers, 1950), 13:32–42.

3. Ibid., pp. 40–41. The complete "economic bill of rights" proposed by President Roosevelt was as follows:

> The right to a useful and remunerative job in the industries or shops or farms or mines of the nation;
>
> The right to earn enough to provide adequate food and clothing and recreation;
>
> The right of every farmer to raise and sell his products at a return which will give him and his family a decent living;
>
> The right of every business man, large and small, to trade in an atmosphere of freedom from unfair competition and domination by monopolies at home or abroad;
>
> The right of every family to a decent home;
>
> The right to adequate medical care and the opportunity to achieve and enjoy good health;
>
> The right to adequate protection from the economic fears of old age, sickness, accident and unemployment;
>
> The right to a good education.

4. Cited in Stephen K. Bailey, *Congress Makes a Law: The Story behind the Employment Act of 1946* (New York: Columbia University Press, 1950), p. 179.

5. Quoted in ibid., p. 42.

6. *Gallup Opinion Index*, no. 38 (July 1968): 23–24; and no. 43 (January 1969): 20–21.

7. U.S. Bureau of the Census, *Current Population Reports*, Series P–60, no. 147, p. 178.

8. Milton Friedman is credited with first popularizing the idea of a "negative income tax," but by the time of the cited Gallup survey, the idea was also being advocated by liberals such as James Tobin and Joseph Pechman. See Milton Friedman, *Capitalism and Freedom* (Chicago: University of Chicago Press, 1962), pp. 190–95; and James Tobin, Joseph A. Pechman, and Peter M. Mieszkowski, "Is a Negative Income Tax Practical?" *Yale Law Journal* 77 (1967): 1–27.

9. In a 1977 Gallup poll, the proposal that "the federal government set up youth camps—such as the CCC camps of the 1930s—for young men who want to learn a trade and earn a little money by outdoor work," was endorsed 85 percent to 10 percent. *Gallup Opinion Index*, no. 138 (January 1977), p. 24. In earlier Gallup polls, similar proposals had been endorsed by 79 percent to 16 percent (1962), 89 percent to 6 percent (1963), and 85 percent to 10 percent (1976). The Gallup polling organization commented on these results, stating, "Few issues in polling history have received such overwhelming support by the American public." Ibid., p. 23.

10. *New York Times*, 1 December 1987.

11. See chapter 6.

12. Public Law No. 95–523, Title I, sec. 102(b), 92 Stat. 1887, 1890 (1978) (codified at 15 U.S.C. § 1021). Cf. ibid., sec. 102(a), and the Employment Act of 1946, Public Law No. 79–304, sec. 2, 60 Stat. 23, 23 (1946).

13. See Philip Alston, "The United Nations' Specialized Agencies and Implementation of the International Covenant on Economic, Social and Cultural Rights," *Columbia Journal of Transnational Law* 18 (1979): 104–05.

14. On the difficulties associated with the monitoring of "promotional" human rights, see Philip Harvey, "Monitoring Mechanisms for International Agreements Respecting Economic and Social Human Rights," *Yale Journal of International Law* 12 (1987): 398–403. Cf. E. W. Vierdag, "The Legal Nature of the Rights Granted by the International Covenant on Economic, Social and Cultural Rights," *Netherlands Yearbook of International Law* 9 (1978): 69.

15. G.A. Res. 2200, 21 U.N. GAOR Supp. (No. 16) at 49, U.N. Doc. A/6316 (1966), art. 2(1).

16. G.A. Res. 2200, 21 U.N. GAOR Supp. (No. 16) at 49, 52, U.N. Doc. A/6316 (1966), art. 2(1).

17. The general view among international jurists is that the Universal Declaration of Human Rights, which was adopted by a vote of the General Assembly of the United Nations, does not impose legally binding obligations on the member states of the United Nations. In this respect, the declaration is distinguishable from the other agreements to which reference is being made, all of which are treaties that legally bind those states (but only those states) that ratify them. On

the other hand, there are jurists who argue that some of the promotional obligations that the declaration proclaims may already have attained, or may be in the process of attaining, legally binding status under customary international law. See, Louis Henkin, "Introduction," in Louis Henkin, ed., *The International Bill of Rights* (New York: Columbia University Press, 1981), p. 9.

18. See chapter 6.

19. See, for instance, Richard A. Posner, *Economic Analysis of Law*, 3d ed. (Boston: Little Brown and Co., 1986).

CHAPTER 1
The Missing Leg of U.S. Social Welfare Policy

1. See, e.g. Herbert Stein, "Still at Work on Full Employment," *Wall Street Journal*, 13 February 1986; or Leonard Silk, "Economic Scene: Looking for Way to Fight Inflation," *New York Times*, 29 July 1988.

2. See Russell A. Nixon, "The Historical Development of the Conception and Implementation of Full Employment as Economic Policy," in Alan Gartner et al., *Public Service Employment: An Analysis of Its History, Problems, and Prospects* (New York: Praeger, 1973), pp. 9–27.

3. William Beveridge, *Full Employment in a Free Society* (New York: W. W. Norton, 1945), p. 18. Beveridge was one of the first advocates of government intervention in the economy to expand employment. See idem, *Unemployment: A Problem of Industry* (London: Longmans, 1909 & 1930). He was also a principal architect of the British welfare state. See idem, *Social Insurance and Allied Services* (New York: Macmillan, 1942).

4. A person must satisfy three conditions to be counted as unemployed in surveys conducted by the U.S. Bureau of Labor Statistics. First, the person must not have done any work at all as a paid employee during the survey week (or more than fifteen hours of unpaid work in an enterprise operated by a member of the family). Secondly, the person must have been available for work, except for temporary illness, during the survey week. Third, the person must have made specific efforts to find employment sometime during the prior four weeks. Thus, a person is counted as unemployed whether the source of his or her joblessness is frictional, cyclical, or structural. On the other hand, job-seekers are not counted as unemployed if they are working in an occupation below their accustomed skill level while seeking a better job, or are working only part-time while seeking full-time work. Also not counted as unemployed are people who report that they want to work but, for whatever reason, are either not currently available for work or are not making specific efforts to find a job. See "Explanatory Notes," *Employment and Earnings* (monthly), or "Notes on Current Labor Statistics," *Monthly Labor Review* (monthly).

5. For general discussions of different types of unemployment, see virtually any labor economics textbook, for instance Ronald G. Ehrenberg and Robert S. Smith, *Modern Labor Economics: Theory and Public Policy*, 3d ed. (Glenview, Ill.: Scott, Foresman & Co.: 1988), pp. 590–605; or Belton M. Fleisher and Thomas J. Kniesner, *Labor Economics: Theory, Evidence, and Policy*, 3d ed. (Englewood Cliffs, N.J.: Prentice-Hall, 1984), pp. 467–72.

6. John Maurice Clark et al., *National and International Measures for Full Employment* (Lake Success, N.Y.: United Nations, 1949), pp. 11, 13.

7. See note 5 above.

8. Clark, *National and International Measures for Full Employment*, p. 14.

9. For discussions of unemployment in the United States before 1890, see Alexander Keyssar, *Out of Work: The First Century of Unemployment in Massachusetts* (Cambridge, Cambridge University Press, 1986); and John A. Garraty, *Unemployment in History: Economic Thought and Public Policy* (New York: Harper & Row, 1978). For estimates of national unemployment rates in the nineteenth century, see Stanley Lebergott, *Manpower in Economic Growth* (New York: McGraw Hill, 1964), pp. 188–89.

10. *Employment and Earnings* 34 (August 1987): 112–16 (table D–1).

11. Ibid. (July 1987): 17 (table A–7), 22 (table A–12).

12. Family Support Act of 1988, Public Law No. 100–485, 102 Stat. 2343 (1988).

13. For a description of the AFDC program, see U.S. Congress, House of Representatives, Committee on Ways and Means, *Background Material and Data on Programs within the Jurisdiction of the Committee on Ways and Means*, 100th Cong., 2d sess., 1988, WMCP 100–29, pp. 387–504.

14. Ibid., pp. 408–10 (table 9), 417 (table 13).

15. For a description of GA programs, see U.S. Department of Health and Human Services, *Characteristics of General Assistance Programs, 1982*, prepared for the Office of Evaluation and Technical Analysis by Urban Systems Research & Engineering, Inc. (May 1983). Other publicly funded income assistance programs are identified in table 2.7.

16. U.S. Bureau of the Census, *Statistical Abstract of the United States: 1988*, 108th ed. (Washington, D.C.: U.S. Government Printing Office), p. 353 (tables 588, 589).

17. *Congressional Record* 134 (29 September 1988): S13639. While most of the changes introduced in the program concern job training and work incentives, the legislation also requires states to take vigorous steps to obtain child support payments from absent fathers and provides the states with new powers to assist them in that effort. See Family Support Act of 1988, Public Law No. 100–485, §§101–29, 102 Stat. 2344–56 (1988).

18. In general, participation in the education and training programs is to be mandatory for AFDC parents who are provided child care and voluntary for those who are not. See ibid., §201, 102 Stat. 2356–60 (1988).

19. The legislation requires states to impose a work requirement of at least sixteen hours per week on at least one parent in two-parent AFDC families whose eligibility for benefits is based on the principal earner's unemployment (about 5 percent of all AFDC families). An exception is allowed for parents under the age of twenty-five who have not completed high school or an equivalent course of education. The work requirement may take the form of (1) on-the-job training, (2) mandatory unpaid community service work performed as a condition for receiving AFDC benefits, or (3) an AFDC subsidized job paying wages in lieu of AFDC benefits. See ibid., 102 Stat. 2376.

20. See ibid., §§302–3, 102 Stat. 2383–93.

21. See "Letter of Transmittal," *Report of the Committee on Economic Security*, 15 January 1935, reprinted in National Conference on Social Welfare, *The Report of the Committee on Economic Security of 1935* (1985), p. 17.

22. Emergency Relief Appropriations Act of 1935, ch. 48, 49 Stat. 115 (1935).

23. Social Security Act of 1935, ch. 531, 49 Stat. 620 (1935).

24. See *Report of the Committee on Economic Security*, pp. 3–7, and the Social Security Act of 1935.

25. *Report of the Committee on Economic Security*, pp. 3–4. William Beveridge was of the same opinion. He saw an effective full employment policy as both a necessary accompaniment to a workable social insurance system and as a desirable goal in its own right. See Beveridge, *Full Employment in a Free Society*, pp. 17–18.

26. *Report of the Committee on Economic Security*, p. 9.

27. Ibid., pp. 8–9.

28. Executive Order No. 7034, 6 May 1935.

29. U.S. National Resources Planning Board, *National Resources Development Report for 1943*, 78th Cong., 1st sess., 1943, Doc. No. 128, Part 3, *Security, Work and Relief Policies*, pp. 236 (table 51), 557–59 (appendix 9).

30. See chapter 6.

CHAPTER 2
The Fiscal Feasibility of Providing Employment Assurance

1. See table 1.2.

2. *Report of the Committee on Economic Security*, 15 January 1935, reprinted in National Conference on Social Welfare, *The Report of the Committee on Economic Security of 1935* (1985), pp. 9–10.

3. See Paul O. Flaim, "Discouraged Workers: How Strong Are Their Links to the Job Market?" *Monthly Labor Review* 107 (August 1984): 8–11.

4. For the age and gender distribution of discouraged workers, see "Household Data Annual Averages," *Employment and Earnings* (January 1978–83), table 39; and (January 1984–87), table 35.

5. See William J. Wilson, *The Truly Disadvantaged: The Inner City, the Underclass, and Public Policy* (Illinois: University of Chicago Press, 1987), pp. 81–106.

6. Over a third of all AFDC families include persons who are not members of the assistance unit. See U.S. Department of Health and Human Services, *Aid to Families with Dependent Children: Recipient Characteristics and Financial Circumstances of AFDC Recipients, 1983* (undated), p. 35 (table 3); and idem, *Aid to Families with Dependent Children: Characteristics and Financial Circumstances of AFDC Recipients, 1986* (undated), p. 31 (table 3). These may include stepparents, stepbrothers and stepsisters, siblings over the age of eighteen, grandparents, and unrelated individuals. Income earned by such persons is not always counted in calculating AFDC eligibility and benefit amounts. See U.S. Congress, House, Committee on Ways and Means, *Background Material and Data on Pro-*

grams within the Jurisdiction of the Committee on Ways and Means, 100th Cong., 1st sess., 1987, WMCP 100–4, pp. 388–89.

7. In 1985 and 1986, about 82 percent of all employed women who maintained families worked full-time. See, *Employment and Earnings* 34 (January 1987): 214–15 (tables 54, 55).

8. On the "security wage" concept as used in New Deal employment programs, see Arthur E. Burns and Edward A. Williams, *Federal Work, Security and Relief Programs*, Works Progress Administration Monograph 24 (1941, reprint ed., New York: DeCapo Press, 1971), pp. 61–63.

9. Part-time workers do, in fact, average about half as many hours worked as full-time workers. See "Household Data Annual Averages," *Employment and Earnings*, (January 1978–83), tables 33, 35; and (January 1984–87), tables 31, 33.

10. For a description of this survey, see Carl Rosenfeld, "Job Search of the Unemployed," *Monthly Labor Review* 100 (March 1977): 40.

11. Otis W. Gilley, "Search Intensity, Reservation Wages, and Duration of Unemployment," *Quarterly Review of Economics and Business* 20 (1980): 104 (table 2).

12. See *Monthly Labor Review* 99 (June 1976): 79 (table 7), 88 (table 17).

13. See sources for table 2.3.

14. See Deptartment of Health and Human Services, *Aid to Families with Dependent Children, 1986*, p. 1; and Committee on Ways and Means, *Background Material* (1987), p. 431 (table 22).

15. See Ralph E. Smith and Bruce Vavrichek, "The Minimum Wage: Its Relation to Incomes and Poverty," *Monthly Labor Review* 110 (June 1987): 24–30.

16. See U.S. Congress, House of Representatives, Committee on the Post Office and Civil Service, *Review of the Federal Employee Health Benefit Program*, 97th Cong., 2d sess., 15 July 1982, p. 13 (table 1).

17. Unpublished data, U.S. Office of Personnel Management, Office of Management and the Budget.

18. Ibid.

19. U.S. Bureau of the Census, *Statistical Abstract of the United States: 1987*, 107th ed. (Washington, D.C.: U.S. Government Printing Office), pp. 421 (table 708), 416 (table 698).

20. Salaries account for between 70 and 80 percent of the cost of providing professional child care. See Dorothy Beers Boguslawski, *Guide for Establishing and Operating Day Care Centers for Young Children* (New York: Child Welfare League of America, 1975), p. 19, and Phyllis Click, *Administration of Schools for Young Children*, 2d ed.(Albany, N.Y.: Delmar Publishers, 1981), p. 125.

21. U.S. Department of Health and Human Services, Office of Human Development Services, *Family Day Care in the U.S.*, vol. 1, *Summary of Findings* (July 1981), p. 38.

22. See Bonnie Fox Schwartz, *The Civil Works Administration, 1933–1934* (Princeton, N.J.: Princeton University Press, 1984), p. 46; John Charnow, *Work Relief Experience in the United States* (Washington, D.C.: Committee on Social Security, Social Science Research Council, 1943), p. 91; and Burns & Williams, *Federal Work, Security and Relief Programs*, pp. 32–33, 57–58, 136–39.

23. These include the Old Age, Survivors, Disability, and Health Insurance programs (OASDHI). What distinguishes these four programs is that they are financed not out of general revenues but by special payroll taxes levied under the authority of the Federal Insurance Contributions Act (FICA). For total OASDHI revenues and expenditures, see *Social Security Bulletin*, (monthly), tables M–4, M–5, M–6, M–7. For a summary report of this data, see *Social Security Bulletin, Annual Statistical Supplement* (annual); or *Statistical Abstract of the United States: 1987*, p. 341 (table 574); and corresponding tables in earlier editions.

24. For data on total government spending, see *Statistical Abstract of the United States: 1987*, p. 249 (table 427); and U.S. Department of Commerce, *Governmental Finances in 1984–85* (1986), p. 1 (table 1).

25. For data on the number of persons living in poverty, see *Statistical Abstract of the United States: 1987*, p. 442 (table 745); and U.S. Bureau of the Census, *Money Income and Poverty Status of Families in the United States: 1986*, Current Population Reports, Series P–60, No. 157 (1987).

26. For annual data on the number of officially unemployed persons, see table 2.1.

27. For total OASDHI contributions by employers, employees, self-employed persons, and the government (in the form of gratuitous wage credits for military service), see *Statistical Abstract of the United States: 1984*, p. 376 (table 615); and *Statistical Abstract of the United States: 1987*, p. 347 (table 584).

CHAPTER 3
Combating Unemployment and Poverty

1. Statement by Robert Taggart in U.S. Congress, House of Representatives, Subcommittee on Crime of the Committee on the Judiciary and Subcommittee on Employment Opportunities of the Committee on Education and Labor, *Unemployment and Crime*, 97th Cong., 1st sess., 27 October 1981, pp. 101–13.

2. See U.S. Congress, Subcommittee on Economic Goals and Intergovernmental Policy of the Joint Economic Committee, *Estimating the Effects of Economic Change on National Health and Social Well-Being*, 98th Cong., 2d sess., 15 June 1984, p. 3.

3. See, for instance, Stephen Platt, "Unemployment and Suicidal Behavior: A Review of the Literature," *Social Science and Medicine* 19 (1984): 93–115.

4. For a review of the literature on this issue, see Belton M. Fleisher and Thomas J. Kniesner, *Labor Economics: Theory, Evidence, and Policy*, 3d ed. (Englewood Cliffs, N.J.: Prentice-Hall, 1984), pp. 497–505.

5. For a discussion of the limitations of the U.S. system of state-operated employment services, see Lloyd Reynolds, *Labor Economics and Labor Relations*, 8th ed. (Englewood Cliffs, N.J.: Prentice-Hall, 1982), pp. 203–07. For a description of the Swedish counterpart to the U.S. system, see Helen Ginsburg, *Full Employment and Public Policy: The United States and Sweden* (Lexington, Mass.: Lexington Books, 1983), pp. 136–44.

6. For a brief description of the job search requirements presently imposed under state unemployment compensation statutes, and for information regarding average benefit levels, see U.S. Congress, House of Representatives, Committee

on Ways and Means, *Background Material and Data on Programs within the Jurisdiction of the Committee on Ways and Means*, 100th Cong., 1st sess., 1987, WMCP 100–4, pp. 332–41.

7. For a general discussion of this point that draws similar policy conclusions to my own, see Adolph Lowe, *Has Freedom a Future* (New York: Praeger, 1988), pp. 95–111.

8. For further discussion of this point, see the discussion of eligibility criteria for an EAP jobs program in chapter 5. For a somewhat dated description of sheltered workshop programs in Europe, see Beatrice G. Reubens, *The Hard to Employ: European Programs* (New York: Columbia University Press, 1970). For a more contemporary description of such programs in Sweden, see Ginsburg, *Full Employment and Public Policy*, pp. 196–205.

9. See William Julius Wilson, *The Truly Disadvantaged: The Inner City, the Underclass, and Public Policy* (Illinois: University of Chicago Press, 1987), pp. 109–24.

10. See U.S. Congress, House of Representatives, Committee on Ways and Means, *Background Material on Poverty*, 98th Cong., 1st sess., 17 October 1983, p. 128. Cf. Bradley R. Schiller, *The Economics of Poverty and Discrimination*, 4th ed. (Englewood Cliffs, N.J.: Prentice-Hall, 1984), pp. 172–73.

11. See, for example, Charles Murray, *Losing Ground, American Social Policy, 1950–1980* (New York: Basic Books, 1984).

12. Sweden provides a singular and very instructive exception to this rule. For a description of Swedish employment policies, see Ginsburg, *Full Employment and Public Policy: The United States and Sweden*, pp. 111–211.

CHAPTER 4
Economic Side Effects of an EAP Jobs Program

1. See Ralph E. Smith and Bruce Vavrichek, "The Minimum Wage: Its Relation to Incomes and Poverty," *Monthly Labor Review* 110 (June 1987): 24–30; Earl F. Mellor, "Workers at the Minimum Wage or Less: Who They Are and the Jobs They Hold," *Monthly Labor Review* 110 (July 1987): 34–41; and Orley Ashenfelter and Robert S. Smith, "Compliance with the Minimum Wage Law," *Journal of Political Economy* 87 (1979): 335–50.

2. See any standard labor economics text, for instance, Ronald G. Ehrenberg and Robert S. Smith, *Modern Labor Economics: Theory and Public Policy*, 3d ed. (Glenview, Ill.: Scott, Foresman and Co., 1988), pp. 77–88; or Belton M. Fleisher and Thomas J. Kniesner, *Labor Economics: Theory, Evidence, and Policy*, 3d ed. (Englewood Cliffs, N.J.: Prentice-Hall, 1984), pp. 77–79.

3. See Charles Brown, Curtis Gilroy, and Andrew Kohen, "The Effect of the Minimum Wage on Employment and Unemployment," *Journal of Economic Literature* 20 (1982): 487–528.

4. For discussions of the price elasticity of the demand for labor in this context, see Fleisher and Kniesner, *Labor Economics*, pp. 79–81. Cf. Ehrenberg and Smith, *Modern Labor Economics*, pp. 105–13.

5. See Fleisher and Kniesner, *Labor Economics*, p. 244. Cf. Ehrenberg and Smith, *Modern Labor Economics*, pp. 460–61.

6. Mellor, "Workers at the Minimum Wage or Less," pp. 35 (table 1), 37 (table 2).

7. See Richard B. Freeman and James L. Medoff, "The Two Faces of Unionism," *The Public Interest* 57 (Fall 1979): 69–93.

8. If the innovation is capable of reducing monetary costs below this level, then a profit-maximizing firm would have introduced it whether or not an increase in wages occurred. In practice, however, it is recognized that a wage increase may have a "shock" effect on employers, inducing them to introduce productivity-enhancing innovations that might have been cost effective even in the absence of the wage increase. See Brown, Gilroy, and Kohen, "The Effect of the Minimum Wage on Employment and Unemployment," pp. 489–90.

9. For a provocative discussion of the importance of rising wages in the process of economic development generally, see Arghiri Emmanuel, *Unequal Exchange* (New York: Monthly Review Press, 1972), pp. 123–42.

10. See any standard textbook on international trade theory, for example, Richard E. Caves and Ronald W. Jones, *World Trade and Payments*, 4th ed. (Boston: Little, Brown & Co., 1985), pp. 11–26.

11. For a concise discussion of the use of incomes policies in the United States, see Ehrenberg and Smith, *Modern Labor Economics*, pp. 656–64.

CHAPTER 5
Administrative Problems and Opportunities

1. See U.S. Bureau of the Census, *Statistical Abstract of the United States: 1987*, 107th ed. (Washington, D.C.: U.S. Government Printing Office), p. 528 (table 902): and tables 2.2 and 2.6 above.

2. See, for instance, George Johnson and James Tomola, "The Fiscal Substitution Effect of Alternative Approaches to Public Service Employment Policy," *Journal of Human Resources* 12 (1977): 3–26; Robert D. Reischauel, "The Economy, the Budget, and the Prospects for Urban Aid," in *The Fiscal Outlook for Cities*, ed. Roy Bahl (Syracuse, N.Y.: Syracuse University Press, 1978), pp. 102–4; Edward M. Gramlich, "State and Local Budgets the Day after It Rained: Why Is the Surplus So High?" *Brookings Papers on Economic Activity* (Washington, D.C.: The Brookings Institution, 1978), no. 1, pp. 191–214. But cf. Michael Wiseman, "Public Service Employment as Fiscal Policy" *Brookings Papers On Economic Activity* (Washington, D.C.: The Brookings Institution, 1976), pp. 67–104; and Michael Borus and Daniel Hamermesh, "Study of the Net Employment Effects of Public Service Employment: Econometric Analysis," in *Job Creation through Public Service Employment*, ed. Richard P. Nathan, et al., 3 vols. (Washington, D.C.: National Commission for Manpower Policy, 1978), 3: 89–149.

3. See, for example, Richard P. Nathan et al., *Public Service Employment: A Field Evaluation* (Washington, D.C.: The Brookings Institution, 1981); and Frederick A. Raffa and Clyde A. Haulman, "The Impact of a PSE Program on Employment and Participants," *Growth and Change* 14 (1983): 14–21.

4. For detailed descriptions of the evolution of the CETA program through the 1970s, see William Mirengoff and Lester Rindler, *CETA: Manpower Programs under Local Control* (Washington, D.C.: National Academy of Sciences, 1978);

William Mirengoff et al., *CETA: Assessment of Public Service Employment Programs* (Washington, D.C.: National Academy of Science, 1980); and William Mirengoff et al., *The New CETA: Effect on Public Service Employment Programs, Final Report* (Washington, D.C.: National Academy of Science, 1980).

5. At its peak CETA funded less than 2.5 million positions, a large proportion of which provided only part-time or summer employment for teenagers. See U.S. Library of Congress, Congressional Research Service, *Cash and Noncash Benefits for Persons with Limited Income: Eligibility Rules, Recipient and Expenditure Data* (annual, 1979–84).

6. The administrators of New Deal employment programs were very much aware of the fiscal substitution problem, and it was one of the factors that caused them to structure the programs the way they did. See John Charnow, *Work Relief Experience in the United States* (Washington, D.C.: Committee on Social Security, Social Science Research Council, 1943), pp. 103–6.

7. See Arthur E. Burns and Edward A. Williams, *Federal Work, Security and Relief Programs*, Works Progress Administration Monograph 24 (1941, reprint ed., New York: DeCapo Press, 1971), pp. 57, 138 (table 7).

8. Ibid., p. 32.

9. See Marilyn Gittell, "Public Employment and the Public Service," in *Public Service Employment: An Analysis of Its History, Problems, and Prospects*, ed. Alan Gartner (New York: Praeger, 1973), pp. 121–42.

10. See Sumner M. Rosen, "Merit Systems and Workers," in *Public Service Employment*, ed. Gartner, pp. 143–53.

11. See Burns and Williams, *Federal Work, Security and Relief Programs*, pp. 29–36, 53–76.

12. See U.S. Congress, House of Representatives, Committee on Ways and Means, *Background Material and Data on Programs within the Jurisdiction of the Committee on Ways and Means*, 100th Cong., 1st sess., 1987, WMCP 100–4, pp. 6–7, 30–34, 505–22.

13. See ibid., pp. 31, 33–39, 505, 534–39.

14. For more detailed discussions of the administrative problems associated with disability determinations, see ibid., pp. 34–53; and Jerry L. Mashaw, *Bureaucratic Justice: Managing Social Security Disability Claims* (New Haven, Conn.: Yale University Press, 1983).

15. *Monthly Labor Review* 110 (November 1987): 65 (table 20).

16. See John Kenneth Galbraith, *The Affluent Society* (Boston: Houghton Mifflin, 1958).

17. Burns and Williams, *Federal Work, Security and Relief Programs*, p. 54 (table 3).

18. Ibid., p. 31 (table 2).

19. For an account of the origins of the CWA, see Bonnie Fox Schwartz, *The Civil Works Administration, 1933–1934* (Princeton, N.J.: Princeton University Press, 1984), pp. 36–39.

20. Employment by all levels of government totaled about 3.2 million at the time. U.S. Bureau of the Census, *Historical Statistics of the United States, Colonial Times to 1970*, (1975), p. 137.

21. Schwartz, *The Civil Works Administration*, pp. 48–50.

22. Burns and Williams, *Federal Work, Security and Relief Programs*, p. 32; and Schwartz, *The Civil Works Administration*, p. 132.

23. Burns and Williams, *Federal Work, Security and Relief Programs*, p. 34; Searle F. Charles, *Minister of Relief: Harry Hopkins and the Depression* (Syracuse: Syracuse University Press, 1963), pp. 48–49, 63–64; Harry Hopkins, *Spending to Save* (New York: W. W. Norton, 1936), pp. 121–22; and Schwartz, *The Civil Works Administration*, pp. 59, 183–85.

24. Schwartz, *The Civil Works Administration*, pp. 58, 69, 135–38, 144–45, 172–78, 183–86; Hopkins, *Spending to Save*, pp. 113, 123; and Burns and Williams, *Federal Work, Security and Relief Programs*, pp. 34–35.

25. Charles, *Minister of Relief*, p. 65.

26. Schwartz, *The Civil Works Administration*, p. 215; and Charnow, *Work Relief Experience in the United States*, p. 99.

27. Private cooperatives of unemployed and underemployed workers emerged spontaneously in 1931 and 1932. First organized to facilitate exchanges of goods and services among the unemployed, several hundred of these associations received federal financial assistance between 1933 and 1938 (but mostly in 1934 and 1935). With this infusion of federal capital, the cooperatives expanded their activities, engaging in regular production and selling their products to relief agencies or exchanging them with other cooperatives. To receive federal funds an association had to be democratic in structure and could not produce goods or services that would significantly affect private markets. Their most common activities were sewing, baking, canning, and gardening, but they also produced furniture, clothing, soap, and cosmetics, and operated laundries, cafeterias, and beauty shops. See U.S. National Resources Planning Board, *National Resources Development Report for 1943*, 78th Cong., 1st sess., 1943, Doc. No. 128, Part 3, *Security, Work and Relief Policies*, pp. 255–58.

28. See Arthur M. Schlesinger, *The Coming of the New Deal* (Boston: Houghton Mifflin, 1958), pp. 277–80.

29. Ibid., pp. 278–79.

30. Ibid., p. 279.

31. See National Resources Planning Board, *Security, Work and Relief Policies*, p. 246.

32. For more information, see Burns and Williams, *Federal Work, Security and Relief Programs*, pp. 58–60.

33. Michael Levy and Michael Wiseman, "An Expanded Public-Service Employment Program: Some Demand and Supply Considerations," *Public Policy* 23 (Winter 1975): 124.

34. This estimate is based on the number of AFDC recipient children under the age of six with an able-bodied parent not already in the laborforce. *Statistical Abstract of the United States: 1986*, p. 382 (table 647).

35. Ibid., p. 357 (table 596).

36. On the origins of the employment at will doctrine, see Jay M. Feinman, "The Development of the Employment at Will Rule," *American Journal of Legal History* 20 (1976): 118–35. The most significant statutory limitations on the em-

ployment at will doctrine are those established by the National Labor Relations Act of 1935, which bars employment discrimination against employees who engage in trade union or other concerted activity, and Title 7 of the Civil Rights Act of 1964, which bars employment discrimination based on race, color, religion, sex, or national origin. For a survey of common law exceptions to the doctrine, see Mark A. Rothstein, Andria S. Knapp, and Lance Liebman, *Employment Law: Cases and Materials* (Mineola, N.Y.: Foundation Press, 1987), pp. 738–858. For contrasting policy arguments regarding the wisdom of the employment at will doctrine, see Richard Epstein, "In Defense of the Contract at Will," *University of Chicago Law Review* 51 (1984): 947–87; and Clyde Summers, "Individual Protection against Unjust Dismissal: Time for a Statute," *Virginia Law Review* 62 (1976): 481–532.

37. See Ed A. Hewett, *Reforming the Soviet Economy: Equality Versus Efficiency* (Washington, D.C.: The Brookings Institution, 1988), pp. 39–42.

38. Cf. John H. Alcorn and David Gleicher, "The Russians Aren't Trying to Be Just Like Us," letter to the editor, *New York Times*, 15 July 1987.

CHAPTER 6
Political Problems

1. See Introduction and discussion of unemployment and social welfare policy in chapter 1.

2. At its peak in the middle of January 1934, the CWA employed 4.26 million persons. The next largest New Deal employment program, the WPA, employed 3.33 million persons at its peak in November 1938. See Arthur E. Burns and Edward A. Williams, *Federal Work, Security and Relief Programs*, Works Progress Administration Monograph 24 (1941, reprint ed., New York: DeCapo Press, 1971), pp. 31 (table 2), 54 (table 3).

3. Before the program's workweek was shortened to save money at the end of January 1934, weekly wages in the CWA averaged $15, or about $65 monthly. When the WPA was established in 1935 it provided average monthly earnings of about $50. Over the eight-year life of the WPA, program wages were slowly increased, but they did not reach $60 per month until 1942. See ibid., pp. 34, 62; and John Charnow, *Work Relief Experience in the United States* (Washington, D.C.: Committee on Social Security, Social Science Research Council, 1943), pp. 51–52.

4. Half of all CWA positions were reserved for persons certified as eligible for public relief, but the other half were open to any unemployed person without submission to a means test. Nine million persons applied for the two million positions available on this basis. See Bonnie Fox Schwartz, *The Civil Works Administration, 1933–1934* (Princeton, N.J.: Princeton University Press, 1984), pp. 42–44. For a comparison of eligibility requirements in different New Deal employment programs, see U.S. National Resources Planning Board, *National Resources Development Report for 1943*, 78th Cong., 1st sess., 1943, Doc. No. 128, Part 3, *Security, Work and Relief Policies*, pp. 556 (appendixes 2, 3, 5), 565 (appendix 13).

5. See Schwartz, *The Civil Works Administration*, pp. 105–16.

6. Harry Hopkins, *Spending to Save* (New York: W. W. Norton, 1936), pp. 123–24.

7. See Burns and Williams, *Federal Work, Security and Relief Programs*, p. 29.

8. See Arthur M. Schlesinger, *The Coming of the New Deal* (Boston: Houghton Mifflin, 1958), pp. 269, 272, 423–24; and Schwartz, *The Civil Works Administration*, pp. 36–37.

9. John Maynard Keynes, "National Self-Sufficiency," *Yale Review* 22 (Summer 1933): 755, 760–61, 763–64.

10. The FERA was established under the authority of the Federal Emergency Relief Act of 1933, ch. 30, 48 Stat. 55 (1933), to distribute federal grants-in-aid to state public relief agencies. For a discussion of its early history, see Burns and Williams, *Federal Work, Security and Relief Programs*, pp. 21–28.

11. The contents of Williams's memo is summarized in Schwartz, *The Civil Works Administration*, p. 36.

12. Ibid., pp. 36–39; George McJimsey, *Harry Hopkins: Ally of the Poor and Defender of Democracy* (Cambridge: Harvard University Press, 1987), pp. 57–58; Schlesinger, *The Coming of the New Deal*, p. 269; and Burns and Williams, *Federal Work, Security and Relief Programs*, pp. 29–30.

13. Quoted in Henry H. Adams, *Harry Hopkins* (New York: G. P. Putnams Sons, 1977), p. 61.

14. Schlesinger, *The Coming of the New Deal*, pp. 8–9, 95, 98, 277, 284–85, 289–93; William E. Leuchtenberg, *Franklin D. Roosevelt and the New Deal: 1932–1940* (New York: Harper and Row, 1963), pp. 84–85; Schwartz, *The Civil Works Administration*, pp. 219–20; and Adams, *Harry Hopkins*, p. 61.

15. Schlesinger, *The Coming of the New Deal*, p. 290; Schwartz, *The Civil Works Administration*, pp. 219–220.

16. See Schlesinger, *The Coming of the New Deal*, p. 271.

17. Investigations of CWA operations by the program's own staff of investigators and accountants ultimately resulted in 751 serious charges being referred to the Justice Department. After completing its own investigation, the Justice Department considered 240 of these cases as warranting further action. Of these, 163 were deemed not to involve criminal violations and were settled through restitution or employee dismissals. Criminal charges were brought in the other seventy-seven cases and seventeen convictions were obtained. See Searle F. Charles, *Minister of Relief: Harry Hopkins and the Depression* (Syracuse: Syracuse University Press, 1963), pp. 59, 63–65.

18. Charles, *Minister of Relief*, pp. 56–58; Schwartz, *The Civil Works Administration*, pp. 89–91.

19. Schwartz, *The Civil Works Administration*, p. 86.

20. Charles, *Minister of Relief*, p. 55; Schwartz, *The Civil Works Administration*, pp. 75–77, 95–101.

21. See discussion of project selection in chapter 5.

22. Schwartz, *The Civil Works Administration*, pp. 216–18.

23. Ibid., p. 216; Charles, *Minister of Relief*, p. 54; Charnow, *Work Relief Experience in the United States*, p. 59; and Schlesinger, *The Coming of the New*

Deal, pp. 217, 274, 485. Roosevelt responded to Governor Talmadge in a letter sent over Hopkins's signature that, "I take it . . . that you approve of paying farm labor 40 to 50 cents per day. . . . Somehow I cannot get it into my head that wages on such a scale make possible a reasonable American standard of living." Ibid., p. 274.

24. Schlesinger, *The Coming of the New Deal*, pp. 273–76; Schwartz, *The Civil Works Administration*, pp. 218–20; Charles, *Minister of Relief*, p. 62.

25. Schlesinger, *The Coming of the New Deal*, p. 273.

26. See Charles, *Minister of Relief*, p. 49; and Charnow, *Work Relief Experience in the United States*, p. 12.

27. Schlesinger, *The Coming of the New Deal*, p. 269.

28. See Schwartz, *The Civil Works Administration*, pp. 42–44.

29. Schlesinger, *The Coming of the New Deal*, p. 273.

30. Ibid., p. 275. On the attitude of the social work profession in general toward the CWA, see Schwartz, *The Civil Works Administration*, pp. 221–25.

31. See Schlesinger, *The Coming of the New Deal*, p. 277; and McJimsey, *Harry Hopkins*, p. 62.

32. Burns and Williams, *Federal Work, Security and Relief Programs*, pp. 30–31, 34; Schwartz, *The Civil Works Administration*, p. 213.

33. See discussion of unemployment and social welfare policy in chapter 1.

34. U.S. National Resources Planning Board, *National Resources Development Report for 1943*, 78th Cong., 1st sess., 1943, Doc. No. 128, Part 1, *Post-War Plan and Program*, pp. 2–3.

35. Ibid., p. 3.

36. Ibid., p. 17.

37. See Introduction.

38. The complete "bill of rights" is reproduced in the Introduction, n. 3.

39. National Resources Planning Board, *Post-War Plan and Program*, pp. 13–17.

40. Message to the Congress on the State of the Union (11 January 1944), reprinted in Samuel I. Rosenman, ed., *The Public Papers and Addresses of Franklin D. Roosevelt*, 13 vols. (New York: Harper & Brothers, 1950), 13:42.

41. Stephen K. Bailey, *Congress Makes a Law: The Story behind the Employment Act of 1946* (New York: Columbia University Press, 1950), p. 27.

42. Ibid., pp. 160–61.

43. Ibid., pp. 37–60. For the text of the original Murray bill, see ibid., pp. 243–48. For a comparison of this text with the earlier staff draft of the bill, see ibid., pp. 56–59.

44. Ibid., pp. 129–49.

45. Ibid., pp. 21–25, 81–92.

46. Ibid., pp. 82, 92–96.

47. See Introduction.

48. Ibid., pp. 180–81.

49. Quoted in Russell A. Nixon, "The Historical Development of the Conception and Implementation of Full Employment as an Economic Policy," in *Public*

Service Employment: An Analysis of Its History, Problems, and Prospects, ed. Alan Gartner (New York: Praeger, 1973), p. 27.

50. Full Employment Bill of 1945, S.380, 79th Cong., 1st sess., §§ 2(b), 2(d)–(e) (1945), reprinted in Bailey, *Congress Makes a Law*, pp. 243–44.

51. U.S. Congress, Senate, War Contracts Subcommittee, Committee on Military Affairs, "A Bill to Establish a National Policy and Program for Assuring Continuing Full Employment," 78th Cong., 2d sess., 18 December 1944, Section 5, quoted in Bailey, *Congress Makes a Law*, p. 58.

52. Employment Act of 1946, Pub. L. No. 79–304, sec. 2, 60 Stat. 23, 23 (1946).

53. For a summary of the bill's provisions, see Helen Ginsburg, *Full Employment and Public Policy: The United States and Sweden* (Lexington, Mass.: Lexington Books, 1983), pp. 64–65.

54. For accounts of the bill's legislative history, see ibid., pp. 65–75; and Harvey L. Schantz and Richard H. Schmidt, "Politics and Policy: The Humphrey Hawkins Story," in *Employment and Labor Relations Policy*, ed. Charles Bulmer and John L. Carmichael (Lexington, Mass.: Lexington Books, 1980), pp. 25–39.

55. Full Employment and Balanced Growth Act of 1978, Pub. L. No. 95–523, Title 1, sec. 102, 92 Stat. 1887, 1890 (1978).

56. Ibid.

57. See Schantz and Schmidt, "Politics and Policy: The Humphrey Hawkins Story," pp. 32–34.

58. Full Employment and Balanced Growth Act of 1978, sec. 104(a)–(c).

59. Ibid., sec. 201.

60. See Introduction.

61. See Ginsburg, *Employment and Public Policy*, pp. 67, 70–71.

62. See Introduction.

63. See, for example, "Paying for Our Dreams: A Budget Plan for Jobs, Peace, and Justice," (Chicago: Jesse Jackson '88, undated).

64. See Paul Simon, *Let's Put America Back to Work* (Chicago: Bonus Books, 1987).

Index

affirmative action, 62–63

Aid for Families with Dependent Children (AFDC): assistance unit characteristics, 122; benefit expenditures, 46–47; earning capacity of AFDC parents, 16–17, 33, 36; estimated participation rate of AFDC parents in an EAP jobs program, 23–29, 31; recent reforms in program, 16–17

American Farm Bureau Federation, 108

American Federation of Labor (AFL), 108–9

American Veterans Committee, 108

anticyclical effect of an EAP jobs program, 25, 56–57

antipoverty policy, 6, 16–20, 63–65

antipoverty program expenditures, 45–51

benefits provided to workers in EAP jobs program, 38–39, 41–44

Beveridge, William, 12, 19n.25

Branion, Ray, 103

business opposition to public employment programs, 91–93, 96, 112–13, 116

California Farm Bureau Federation, 104

Chamber of Commerce, 104, 108

child care, 23, 41–43, 50, 85, 91, 94, 125

Civilian Conservation Corps, 4n.9, 86, 95, 102

Civil Rights Act (1964), 96n.36

civil rights organizations, 10, 108, 113

Civil Works Administration (CWA), 86, 89–91, 99–106, 108

Clark, John Maurice, 12–13

Committee for Constitutional Government, 108

Committee on Economic Security (1935), 18–20, 22, 30, 106, 111

Comprehensive Employment and Training Act (CETA), 79–83

Congress of Industrial Organizations (CIO), 108–9

countercyclical effect of an EAP jobs program, 25, 56–57, 76

crime and unemployment, 52

Cummings, Homer, 18

Dewey, Thomas E., 4

Disability Insurance program (DI), 87

disabled persons: current benefit payments for, 46–47; their eligibility for income maintenance benefits following establishment of an EAP jobs program, 22, 45, 87–88; and public support for benefit payments to the disabled, 64; and support services provided by EAP jobs program for partially disabled workers, 43, 61–62, 86

discipline. *See* worker discipline

discouraged workers, 24–28, 31, 33

Douglas, Lewis, 102, 105

drug and alcohol abuse, 43, 98

earned income tax credit, 36, 123

economic bill of rights, 4n.3, 106–7

economic planning, 75

efficiency: effect of an EAP jobs program on, 70–75

eligibility criteria for income maintenance benefits following establishment of an EAP jobs program, 18–20, 22–23, 45, 87–88

Emergency Relief Appropriations Act (1935), 18–19

employee recruitment by private employers, 54–56, 59

Employment Act (1946), 5, 8, 106–11, 114–15

Employment Assurance Policy (EAP): as an antipoverty measure, 63–65; current proposal defined, 5, 21–23; and economic efficiency, 70–75; effectiveness of, in combating unemployment, 53–63, 66–70; effect of, on public-sector labor relations, 85–86; effect of, on wage rates generally, 66–70; and fiscal substitution, 79–86, 93; inflationary effect of, 75–78; net cost of policy, 43–44, 48–50; and New Deal proposals, 18–20, 99–101, 105–7; political opposition to, 99–117; and project selection, 40–43, 84–86, 88–96; and worker discipline, 71–72, 96–98